PROCESS OF URBAN PEOPLING

Dr. Sangeeta Boruah Saikia

Dedicated to my father

Late Purna Kanta Boruah

an engineer and a writer

Contents

1. Physical Setting

2. Cultural Bases

3. Economic Bases

5. Process of Growth and Development

6. Process of Migration

7. Demography, Social and Occupational Status of Urban Centres

List of Tables

List of Figures

List of Abbreviations

AMCH   -   Assam Medical College Hospital

AOC   -   Assam Oil Corporation

AOD   -   Assam Oil Division

APL   -   Assam Petrochemical Limited

ARATC   -   Assam Railway and Trading Company

ASEB   -   Assam State Electricity Board

ASTC   -   Assam State Transport Corporation

ATR-   -   Assam Trunk Road

BCPL-   -   Brahmaputra Cracker and Polymer Limited

BPCL   -   Bharat Petroleum Corporation Limited

BVFC   -   Brahmaputra Valley Fertilizer Corporation

CIL   -   Coal India Limited

LP-   -   Lower Primary

LPG   -   Liquid Petroleum Gas

IOC   -   Assam Oil Division

IWT   -   Inland Water Transport

MB   -   Municipal Board

NH   -   National Highway

NHAI   -   National Highways Authority of India

SC   -   Schedule Caste

SSI   -   Small Scale Industry

ST   -   Schedule Tribe

TC   -   Town Committee

TE   -   Tea Estate

Preface

Urbanisation is a social and economic process that has sharply taken into shape and intensified in the concentration of the population and settlement at a certain point of high concentration of economic activities developed during the age of modern technology. The process of Urbanisation reflects the increase of town-living people as well as an increase in the number of urban centers and extension of urban activities and way of life in a region obviously with the associated decrease of the percentage of rural population and activities. The study of urban geography is an important field for geographers of today's concern in development studies, which is, of course, largely a product of the twentieth century.

Dibrugarh and Tinsukia Districts, previously constituting the Dibrugarh District is an emerging urbanized area next to the Kamrup District area located between 27°5$^{/}$ N and 27°58$^{/}$ N and 94°35$^{/}$E and 96°0$^{/}$E in the easternmost part of Assam south of the Brahmaputra. It is the area where modern life started first in Assam through the establishment of tea gardens and coal and oil industries. First railway lines and trunk roads were initiated in this area during the colonial era laying the ground for modern urbanization. It covers a total area of 7171 km^2 consisting mostly of plains with scattered hills and hilly areas in its eastern and southern margins bordering Arunachal Hills. Since the British period, the area has been a place for urban growth, though the process is a slower one. Dibrugarh and Tinsukia Districts have been a functional coherence since the time of the development of the transport network and associated modern industrial and commercial activities, so it is legitimate to consider these two present districts as a single unique one. The two districts have inseparable functional coherence and unique interdependence in respect of the process of urbanization since its inception. But despite the presence of abundant resources and infrastructure in the districts, the emerging trend of urbanization is not satisfactory and also the development process of the districts is not fast. So it requires proper investigation in the process of urban peopling for growth of urban centers and regional development.

The organization of book is divided into seven chapters. Chapter one begins with a discussion on the Physiography, Geological Formation, Climate, and Natural Vegetation of the Dibrugarh and Tinsukia Districts. The cultural and economic basis of the districts has been analysed in chapter two and three. Chapter four and five have been made, presenting a systematic and comprehensive analysis of the population characteristics of urban centres and their process of growth and development. Lastly Chapter six and seven contains a discussion on the process of peopling, demography, and social and occupational status of urban centres.

I would like to acknowledge with a deep sense of respect and sincere gratitude to Dr. Bhuban Gogoi, former Principal and

HOD of the Geography Department of Tinsukia College for his ungrudging guidance, valuable suggestions, and improvement of the writing of this work.

I am extremely thankful to my colleague Mr. Narendra Kr. Das for cartographic works and numerous suggestions provided to me along with Dipangka Dutta for sincere help in completing the book. I am obliged to record my special thanks to my mother, and my family members for their assistance especially my husband Mr. Diganta Saikia has as ever been my greatest source of strength without his constant cooperation and moral support I could not have done my work.

Lastly, I extend due respect and gratitude to all whose help and co-operations will be valuable to me all the time.

Dr. Sangeeta Boruah Saikia

I PHYSICAL SETTING

An Introduction to Dibrugarh and Tinsukia Districts:-

The Dibrugarh and Tinsukia Districts (formerly the unified Dibrugarh district) are located in upper Assam's featureless, flat Brahmaputra valley's easternmost section (fig- 1.1). The Dibrugarh and Tinsukia districts with the second-highest urban population, behind Kamrup District,where the Guwahati Metropolitan City is located. The British introduced the modern way of life to Assam by establishing the coal, tea, and oil industries here and connecting them to the transportation network. The districts are important for the development of the modern economy and as a focal point for national security. It is located at the top of the Brahmaputra Valley, and the Brahmaputra River, which divides the Dibrugarh, Tinsukia, and Lakhimpur, Dhemaji districts on the north, borders it on the north and north-west. Arunachal Pradesh borders it in the north, east, and southeast. Sibsagar district borders it on the southwest. The area is a portion of a large plain that logically rises to the base of the hills and offers a varied landscape. The hills to the south of the area are only a few thousand feet above mean sea level, whilst the hills to the east are much higher and can be seen as a continuous chain of snowy peaks on clear winter days. Except for a few stray hills in the Makum and Buri Dihing mauzas of the Margherita sub-division, the districts are a flat, level plain that

LOCATION OF DIBRUGARH AND TINSUKIA DISTRICTS

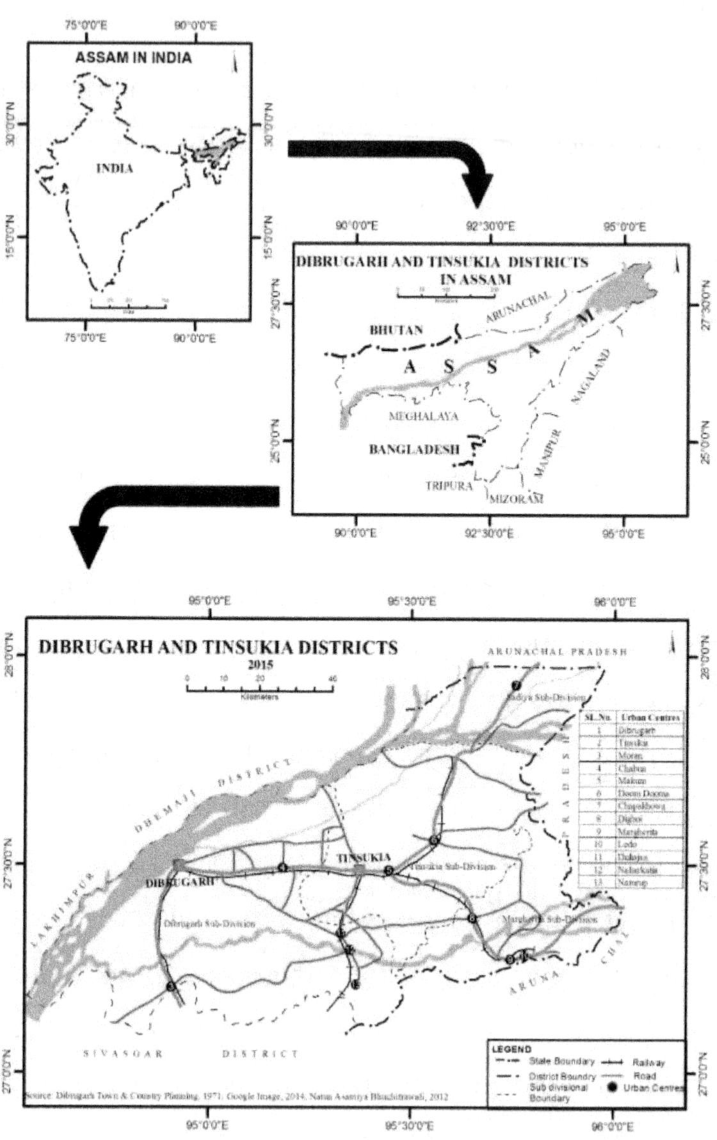

Fig-1.1

stretches from the Disang river through the south of Joipur and Tipling mauzas.

Before 1979, there was just one Dibrugarh district, which was a part of the former Lakhimpur District of Assam. The Dibrugarh and Tinsukia districts now make up two districts in Upper Assam. Up until 1979, the headquarters of these two districts, which together made up the former Dibrugarh district, were in Dibrugarh Town. After that, the Tinsukia district was created, with Tinsukia Town serving as its administrative centre. As a result, this district includes the Tinsukia and Dibrugarh districts' headquarters towns. The 7171 km^2 Dibrugarh and Tinsukia districts are situated between 27°5$^/$ N and 27°58$^/$ N and 94°35$^/$E and 96°0$^/$E. To analyse the geographical context of urbanisation, several geographical elements must be taken into account in the following.

Physiography:-

The easternmost region of the Brahmaputra plain—the Dibrugarh and Tinsukia Districts—is higher and wider than other areas of the valley, and the foothills at the border are the highest and most heavily forested.It is situated at the head of the Brahmaputra valley where the huge Brahmaputra River flows in the north. Many hillocks and hills in the region's extreme south rise from a few hundred feet high in the southwest to close to a thousand feet high in the southeast above the plain's typical ground level.

The principal rivers which fall into the Brahmaputra in the Dibrugarh and Tinsukia districts are the Buri-Dihing, Lohit, Kundil, Dibru, and Dibang. These rivers flow mostly in a north-westerly direction whereas some towards the west and south-westerly direction course. Thus the general slope of the districts is towards the north and northwest flanked by the lofty Patkai range located at the distant south and the southeast international border of Arunachal Pradesh with Myanmar. Towards the flowing direction of the Brahmaputra, the average elevation of the region is 134 metres at Sadiya in the east and 104 metres at Dibrugarh in the west above the mean sea level having a slope almost of 20cm per km. towards west. The Dibrugarh and Tinsukia districts can be divided into two broad divisions (1) the Brahmaputra plain and (2) the south and south-eastern foot-hills region (fig-1.2) as discussed in the following.

1) Brahmaputra Plain:-This plain comprises thick alluvial soil of later tertiary and quaternary age. The tertiary deposits are consisting mainly of sandstone, shale, grit, conglomerate, and limestone and the quaternary ones are alluvial sediments comprising pebbles, sand, and silt. Because of the alluvial soil and its fertility, the Brahmaputra plain has always evolved human interest. Based on tributary basins and physiographic character, the

Brahmaputra plain can be subdivided into (a) the Sadiya plain and (b) the Brahmaputra active flood plain. (c) Dibru plain and (d) Burhi- Dihing plain.

a) Sadiya Plain:- It's a tiny area of land in the northeast. Being as enormous as the Brahmaputra, the Luhit and the Dibang encircle and separate the Sadiya (called the "Rukmini plain" by Borthakur in 1968) from the mainland. This land unit is traversed by the tributary known as the Kundli. The slightest impediment causes all of the rivers in this area to change their flow. Where rivers travel over a level plain with a little gradient, oxbow lakes meander and marshy areas frequently form along with their courses. During the monsoon season, these areas commonly experience flooding, which often results in residents' loss of life and property. River bank erosion happens often throughout the year, primarily during the monsoon season.

This region suffered significant damage from the big earthquake of 1950, whose epicenter was only 380 kilometres east of the districts. Floods, bank erosion, and channel shifting have now become frequent occurrences in the Districts' rivers. Significant amounts of silt have built up in the riverbeds, and numerous waterways have altered their paths. As a result of the earthquake, the former cities of Saikhowa Ghat and Sadiya were consumed by the Dibong and the Brahmaputra through their rapid bank erosion.

Dibrugarh And Tinsukia Districts
Physiographic Divisions
N
Sadiya Plain
Brahmaputra Plain
Dibru Plain
Burhi Dihing Plain
South & South Eastern
Foothill Region
Kilometers
Source: Borooah, 1985, Bhagabati, Borah & Kar, 2002, etc.

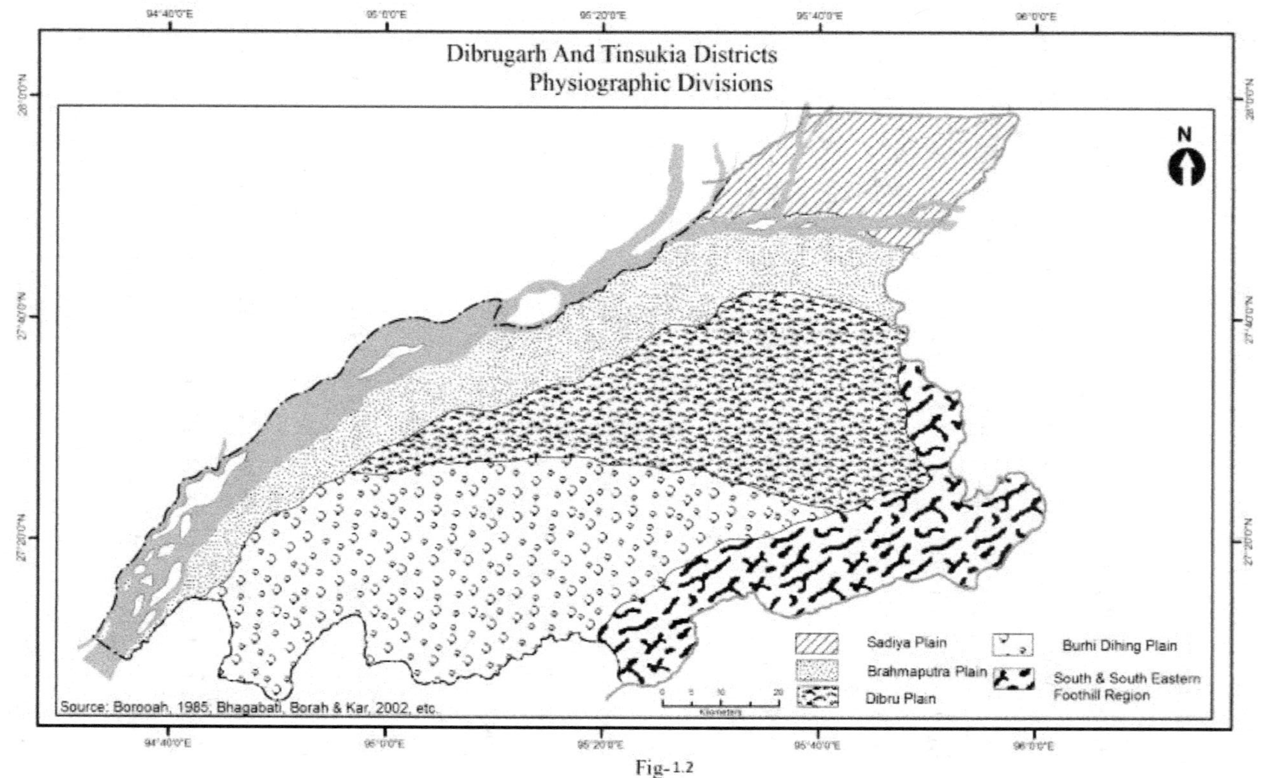

Fig-1.2

b) Brahmaputra Active Flood Plain: - This area of land stretches from the confluence of the Noa Dihing with the Lohit in the northeast to the confluence of the Burhi-Dihing with the Brahmaputra in the west along the bank of the Lohit and the Brahmaputra. The Brahmaputra is being continuously under the process of siltation and there the occurrence of braiding and widening of its course has happened. Bank erosion and siltation go on side by side whereas the latter with less intensity in the course. After the great earthquake of 1950, bank erosion, especially along the left bank has become a regular feature. The Brahmaputra has silted up its bed by about 2.5 to 3 metres. The extent of channel shifting and bank erosion at Dibrugarh was tremendous and the river has been eating up almost the whole of the original site of Dibrugarh town since 1911. Recently Dibong-Lohit combined channel bifurcates from the main channel and flows south of the Dibru-Saikhowa national park to meet the Brahmaputra at Rohmoria. Inspite of flood havoc, earthquakes, etc. the river basins and sub-basins have been always attractive points of human habitation since historical times. These places create the foundation for both rural and urban settlements based on subsistence farming, forest products, tea gardens, and other district resources.

c) Dibru Plain: - A tributary of the Brahmaputra is the river Dibru. It drains the districts' northeastern region. It originates from a short hilltop that is 500 feet (152 metres) high or less on the

Dibrugarh And Tinsukia Districts
Drainage Pattern
N
ARUNACHAL PRADESH
DHEMAJI DISTRICT
LAKHIMPUR
SIVASAGAR DISTRICT
Lohit
Kundil
Dibang
Dhola
Brahmaputra
Burhi Dehing
Tipam
Digboi
Disoi
Source: Satellite Imagery, 2014; Borooah, 1985; Gogoi, 2008, etc.
Kilometers

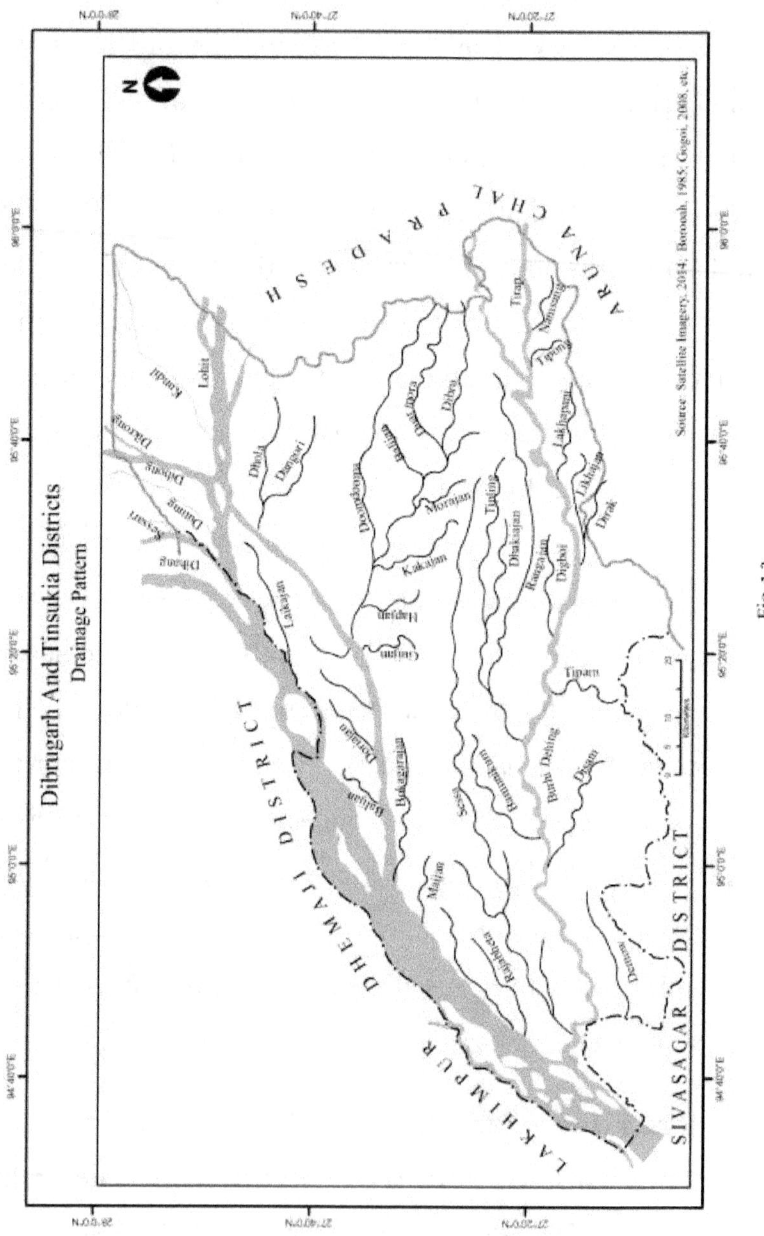

Fig-1.3

eastern edge of the districts, not far from the Burhi Dihing valley, and it runs westward through the districts. It is known in some parts of the upper course as the Doom Dooma river where the Doom Dooma river joins it and in the lower course as the Dibru river where some parts in Tinsukia are known as Guijan. Its lower part is captured by the recently flowing Dibang-Lohit combined avulsion channel converting it to be a part of the Brahmaputra. Its important tributaries are Kakajan, Moranjan, Hapjan, Balijan, Duarmora, etc. All of these drainage channels have varying straight, meandering, and intertwining paths. On the high grounds of the former alluvium, there are clearly defined changing channels, river captures, ox-bow lakes, lowlands, and swamps that are either covered by vast tea gardens or a few reserve kinds of wood.

On average, the Dibru plain measures 19 km in width and 96 km in length. Although the valley is formed by an agriculturally productive plain, the lower and northeastern portions are frequently subject to fluvial regimes that include flooding, deposition, bank erosion, etc., making them unsuitable for steady human activity.

d) Buhi Dihing Plain: - Another significant tributary to the Brahmaputra, the Burhi Dihing has a significantly more twisting course than the Dibru and has the greatest basin area among the districts. The entirety of the district's southern portion is covered by its basin plain. The river rises in upper Myanmar, travels through the Patkai Range, reaches the districts, flows slowly via several meanders, and finally empties into the Brahmaputra. The river left behind numerous oxbow lakes, also known as "beel" in the local language, dry channels, and marshes on both sides. Moreover, it has several significant tributaries, including Digboi, Tipling, Tingrai, Sessa, Tirap, Namchik, Dirak, etc. (fig. 1.3).interestingly all from the north and there are no major tributaries in its south bank except minor ones like Disam, Tipam, Dirak, Likhajan, Lekhapani, Tipong, Namsang, etc.

The Burhi- Dihing basin plain in the districts is bordered by the hills in the east and south-east and by the undefined water divide line between the Dibru basin and the Burhi-Dihing basin through which the Dibru-Sadiya railway line passes in parts in the north. Its eastern part from Margherita eastward is a plain embayed into the Tirap Hills created by valley extension through lateral erosion. Westward from a strip of this embayment up to about Jaipur, the plain rests on erosional-cum depositional platform with relatively high ground and numerous low hillocks rising occasionally up to a height of about 300 metres. Such hillocks form a common feature in the natural landscape of Margherita, Digboi, Burhi Dihing, Makum, Jaipur, and Tipling Mauzas. The western part of the plain is flat and low-lying with the shifting courses of the river as mentioned above.

The loose, loamy soil that makes up the basin plain makes it simple for the river to cut its soft banks, particularly its south bank. Moreover, it has frequent fluvial regimes of flooding. It's one of the reasons Naharkatia and Joipur are the only notable urban centres in the southern portion of the lower Burhi Dihing valley, which is less populous overall. On the other hand, the area over the water divide of the Dibru valley and the Burhi- Dihing valley is highly populated and is the most important tract with the maximum number of developed and potential urban centres in the districts. The vital economic significance and recent urban development of the districts have been greatly linked to this part, particularly after the recent discovery of oil-bearing beds in this part of the Burhi Dihing plain.

2) The Foothills of the South and South East:-

This unit is responsible for the districts over Jaipur, Margherita, and Digboi Thanas in their southern and southern-eastern portions. This district is about 150 meters high on average and its elevation gradually increases to the east of Ledo with a maximum of 530 meters.

In the southwest and northeast trend, there are five ranges of hills distinguished in these districts. They are Hilika Parbat (maximum height of 465 meters) and Khathalguri Parbat (230 meters) in Jaipur Thana and Lompi Parbat, Tikak Parbat (493 meters), and Yuting Takkan (530 meters) in Margherita Thana. Apart from these hill ranges, there exist a few isolated hillocks in the Makum and Burhi Dihing mauzas.

Dibrugarh And Tinsukia Districts
Geology and Tectonics
N
Formation
Geological Time
Alluvium   Recent/ Pleistocene
Dihing   Plio Pleistocene/ Mio Pliocene
Tipam   Miocene
Barail Series   Oligocene
Disang   Eocene
Naga Thrust
Margherita Dihing Thrust
Haflong Disang Thrust
Source: Taher & Ahmed, 2001; Dutta & Dutta, 1976 and Borooah, 1985.

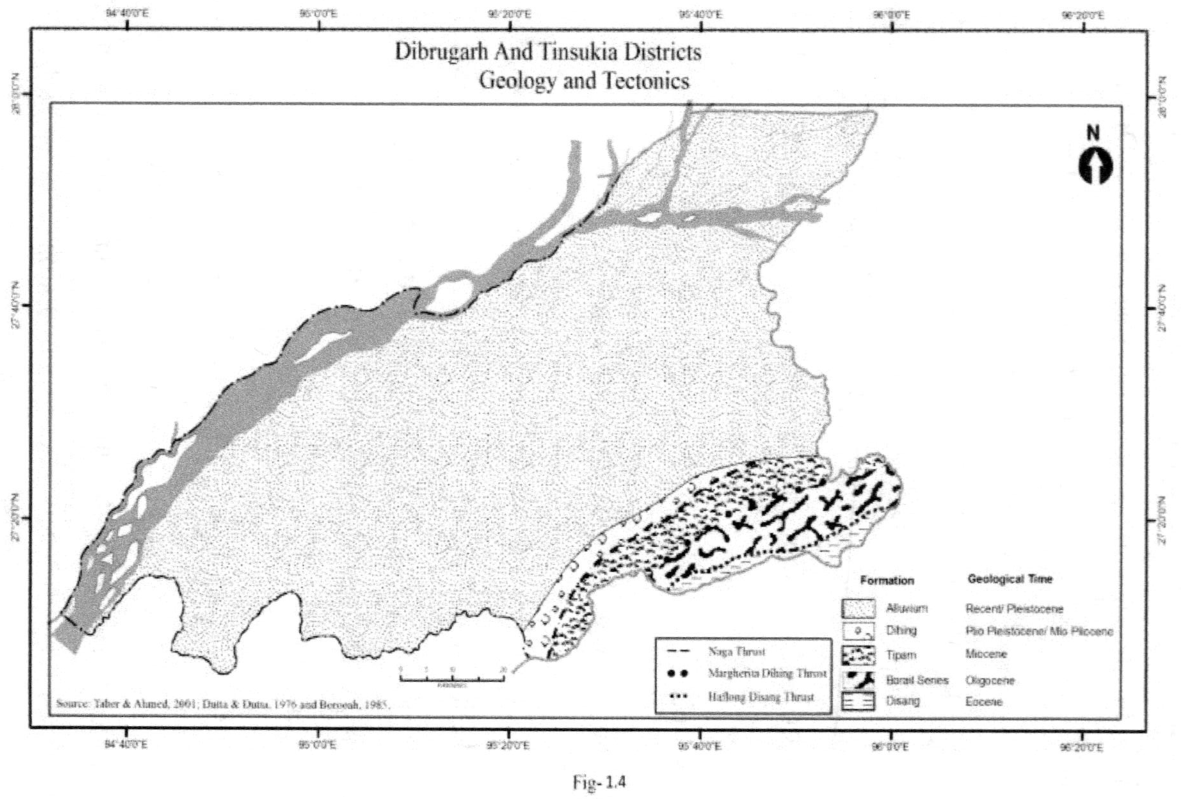

Fig- 1.4

Geological Formation:

Geological Formations and Succession of Beds:-

Under the loose soil, the districts have a notably thick group of sedimentary rocks. These rocks, which span the geological time scale (fig. 1.4) from Eocene (Early Tertiary) to Pleistocene (Post Tertiary), are mostly exposed along the foothills that form the districts' south-eastern border. Along the Himalayan foothills over the northern boundary, only the upper parts of the group of rocks are seen along a narrow fringe following the base of the hills up to Nizamghat. In the eastern part and along the valley of the Brahmaputra, the rock formations are covered by thick alluvial deposits belonging to sub-recent and recent periods. The following series and stages are the tertiary groups of rocks in this area, according to their chronological order of superposition, the eldest being at the bottom (table-1.1).

Table -1.1
Dibrugarh and Tinsukia Districts Region
Geological Succession of Beds

Era	Age	Series	Stage	Thickness
Quaternary Era	Recent	New alluvium	Newer or low level alluvium	
		Unconformity		
-do-	Pleistocene	Old alluvium	Older or high level alluvium	
		Unconformity		
Tertiary	Plio-pleistocene	Dihing series	Dihing or Dhekiajuli	300-400m
		Unconformity		
do-	Mio-pliocene/Pliocene	Dupitila	Namsang/Dupitila stage	800m
		Unconformity		

-do-	Miocene	Tipam Series	Girujan clay stage ———— 900m-
-do-	————	-do-	Tipam Sandstone stage 1400m -
do-	————	Surma	Surma Sandstone
		Unconformity	
-do-	Oligocene	Barail Series	Tikak Parbat Stage ———— 550m
-do-	————	————	Bargolai Stage ——— 2500m
-do-	————	————	Naojan Stage ——— 1000m
		Unconformity	
-do- faults	Eocene and Mesozoic Palaeocene	Jaintia and Disang Series	Kapili Alteration obscured by Sylhet Limestone
		Unconformity	
Palaeozoic Pre-Cambrian Granitic Rock Basement (Shillong group) not classified			
		Unconformity	
Archaeozoic	Archaean	Archaean	not classified

Sources:Geological Survey of India Report,Goswami-1963;Dehadrai,1973;Director General's Report 1974;Baruah & Rahman 1976; Das Gupta,1979- and Gazetteer of India, Assam, Lakhimpur District by K.N. Dutta and N.C.Dutta,1976,(Compiled by the author).

1. The Jaintia Disang series, a thick succession of hard and sand-filled shale, makes up the Tertiary Group. The Haflong-Disang thrust fault is pushing the younger Barails, Surmas, and Tipams over into the high hills covered in Disang shale that is located behind the southern boundary of the Makum coalfield.

2. The Barail series will come after. The Naojan stage is a representation of its lowest portion. The region south and southwest of Namsang at the edge of the Haflong-Disang thrust is covered in Naojan sandstones. This stage's rock beds are well exposed along the Margherita-Changlang road, the upper courses of the Namsang, Ledo, and Tipangpani rivers, and behind the Namsang colliery of the Makum coalfield to the south of the thrust.

3. The Borgolai stage, which consists of calcareous and carbonaceous shale with numerous thin, unworkable coal seams, represents the middle section of the series. On the northern highlands between Dirak and Ledo, in the Makum coalfield region, the stage is primarily exposed. There are multiple oil seeps and oil-bearing sandstone horizons in this stage.

4. The upper section of the series is represented by the Tikak Parbat stage, which consists of sandy shale, shale clays, and carbonaceous shale with multiple thick seams of coal at the base. The stage spans between Namsang and the former Tirap colliery and completely encircles the Tikak hill of the Makum coalfield.

5. Variable ratios of sandstone, clay, shale, quartz, and fossils can be found in the Tipam Sandstone Stage, which is the bottom portion of the series. The Tipam Sandstone covers the centre section of the Namsang syncline and spreading towards the east, covers the ridge of the Tikak-Ledo-Tipam and Hanju range of hills. The majority of the Jaipur-Tipam-Digboi range of hills is covered by another belt of Tipam sandstones.

6. A substantial group of mottled clays serves as a representation of the series' overlying Girujan clay stage. The Girujan clays cover the low-lying hills to the east and northeast of the Makum Coalfield, which are flanked on the south by the Jaipur-Tipam-Digboi range of hills.

7. The Namsang stage is composed of alternating beds of soft conglomeratic sandstones that range in colour from bluish to greenish-grey.

8. From the Burhi Dihing river's junction with the Namchick river up until that point, the Dihing series is well exposed. This series creates low mounds in the eastern section, which are encircled by earlier alluvium.

From the preceding description, it is clear that the southern portion of these districts has a reservoir of coal, petroleum, and natural gas. For this reason, the production of mineral resources gives the districts' industrial development a unique boost that we cannot find in any other part of Assam.

Geo-Physical Micro-units:-

Three geophysical units can be separated into districts based on physiographic and geological formations. (1) Alluvial plain (2) Old alluvial plain, and (3) Piedmont plain (fig.1.5). Continuously away from the Brahmaputra and the Lohit, the landform micro-units are the New alluvial plain, Old alluvial plain, and Piedmont plain. The altitude increases in the same direction as per the above pattern of distribution of landforms. The geological formation is also continually changing as it approaches the Lohit and Brahmaputra. Mineral resources are concentrated in areas that are accessible and conducive to exploration in the older geological strata.

Soil:-

The Brahmaputra, Dibru, and Burhi Dihing rivers and their tributaries are primarily responsible for eroding and depositing alluvial soils on the land surface of the Dibrugarh and Tinsukia districts. The alluvial soil by rivers is often sandy, while it is typically clayey away from rivers. These alluvial soils are composed of both old and recent alluvium. The piedmont and foothill region in the south and southeast of the districts also have hilly lateritic soil (fig-1.5).

The early stages of the late Pleistocene and modern times saw the deposition of the ancient alluvium. Due to tectonic activity, it gradually rises to a relatively higher level over time. This soil is less fertile, more acidic, and more compacted. It also has lower levels of phosphate and potash. The type of soil is found generally in the middle courses of the Burhi Dihing, Dibru, Kundli, and Dibang. These deposits contain alternating beds of pebble, gravel, or boulder with loose sand and clays. Many of the low mounds along the valley of the Burhi Dihing in Margherita, Digboi, and Jaipur Thanas are entirely made up of old alluvial deposits. The old alluvium has a relatively high percentage of acid and soluble Mg accompanied by Ca. In general, its IICI soluble

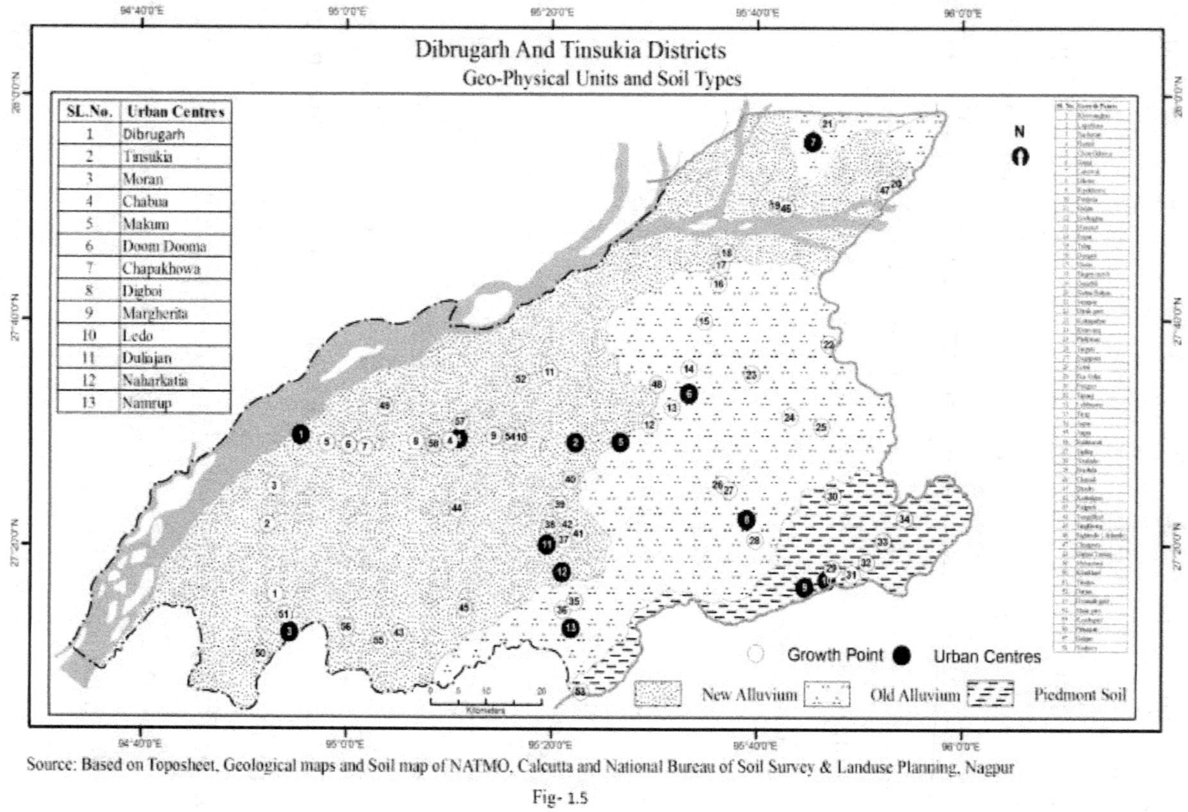

SL.No.	Urban Centres
1	Dibrugarh
2	Tinsukia
3	Moran
4	Chabua
5	Makum
6	Doom Dooma
7	Chapakhowa
8	Digboi
9	Margherita
10	Ledo
11	Duliajan
12	Naharkatia
13	Namrup

Source: Based on Toposheet, Geological maps and Soil map of NATMO, Calcutta and National Bureau of Soil Survey & Landuse Planning, Nagpur

Fig- 1.5

material contents are lower. The P^H value is also between 4.2 to 5.5 percent with very low quality of exchangeable calcium which varies from 0.1 to 5 mg per 100 grams of soil (Borooah, 1985).

The early stages of the late Pleistocene and modern times saw the deposition of the ancient alluvium. Due to tectonic activity, it gradually rises to a relatively higher level over time.This soil is less fertile, more acidic, and more compacted. It also has lower levels of phosphate and potash.

The new alluvial soil is rich in organic matter and is made up of silt and sand that have just been dumped. As a result, even if it is not entirely sandy, this type of soil is rich and good for farming. This soil is generally rich in Phosphate, Potash, Calcium, Nitrogenous material, and organic substances. It is less acidic and not saline. It is Chemical and Physical characteristics, however, vary to some extent from place to place. New alluvium is found in the vast plain of the districts right across the valleys of the Burhi Dihnig, Sessa, Lohit, Kundil, Dibru, Brahmaputra, and Dibang extending in the south-western part from the north-eastern borders of the districts close to the rivers. The young built-up plain and the active flood plain zone are often the areas of new alluvium. The majority of this soil is made up of black mud, which ranges in depth from 0.6 to 1.2 metres and sits on a hard clay subsurface. The new alluvial soils discovered away from the river are physically silty loam. However, those close to the river banks have a high sand content and turn into sandy loam (Borooah,1985).

In comparison to the old alluvium, the new alluvium is less acidic. It has a range of 5.5 to mildly alkaline P^H values. These soils have high levels of PO_4K, and Ca (6 to 21 mg per 100 g of soil), but their N_2 content is only 0.1 percent, which is only moderate (Borooah, 1985). The piedmont zone contains lateral soils in the Makum, Digboi, and Margherita regions. This soil lacks potash, phosphoric acid, lime, and potash and is black, finely grained, and heavy loam.

Tectonics:-

The districts have comprised a wide alluvial tract and it geomorphologically reflects the eastern end of a big trough or "Fore Deep" of tectonic origin. The Shillong plateau, which lies tucked between the Patkai and Himalayan hills and is now covered in several thousand metres of gravel and alluvium, extends eastward into this depression (Dutta and Dutta, 1976).

The early Cretaceous and Tertiary bedrock of the depressions that had developed in these regions as a result of tectonic upheaval have been covered by the deposition of alluvial sediments, creating the Brahmaputra plain. Although the Brahmaputra trough's origin is unknown, it is believed to be the result of the Indian plate's frontal portion down buckling as a result of plate tectonic events that have been forcing it northward down the central Asian plate.

N.E. India and Adjacent Regions
Epicenters and Magnitudes of Earthquakes

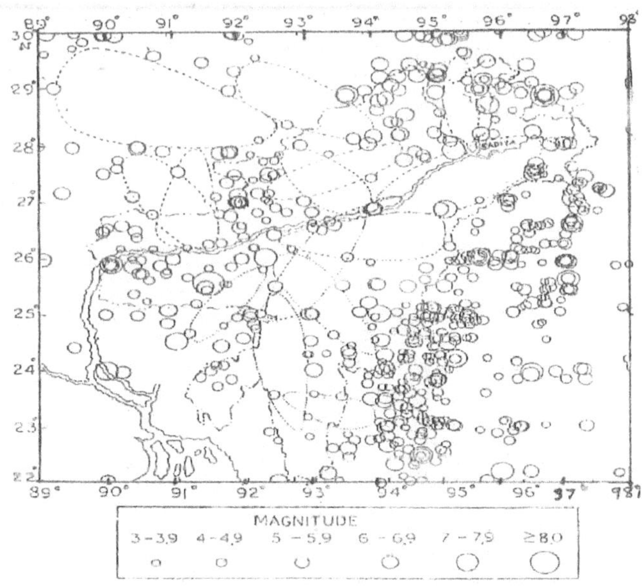

Source: Seismological Survey of India, Shillong
Fig-1.6 (a)
The Earthquake of 1897

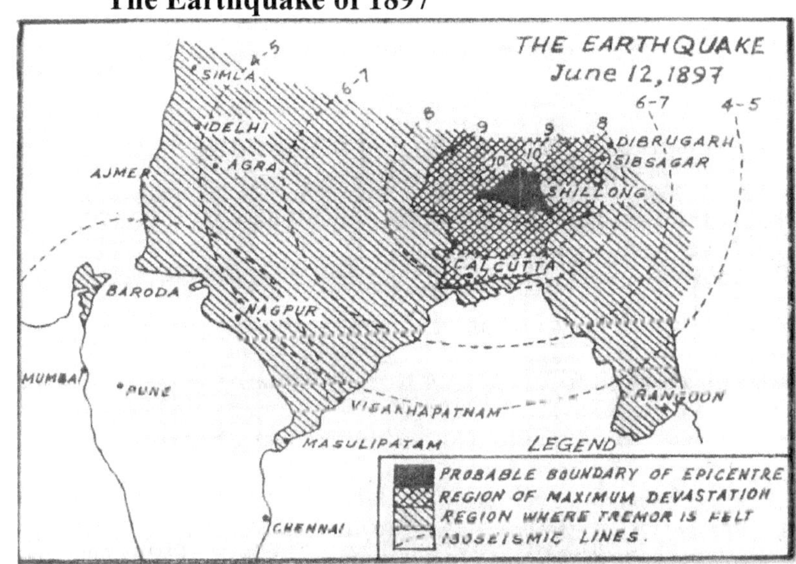

Fig 1.6 (b)
Source: Seismological Survey of India, Shill

The districts are highly sensitive to the tectonic activities of earthquakes. It is one of the highest earthquake-prone zones in the world. Great earthquakes did occur in the region as a whole in 1897 and 1950 to the magnitude of 8.7 Richter scale (fig-1.6 (a) and 1.6 (b).

Climate:-

Sub-tropical monsoon weather can be seen in the districts of Tinsukia and Dibrugarh. Dibrugarh is completely exposed to the monsoon winds that carry moisture. Throughout the entire year, winds are typically low and primarily come from the north and east. The relative humidity in the air is typically around 70% all year long, making it exceedingly humid. Skies are heavily clouded to overcast in the southeast monsoon summer season. In the post-monsoon and cold seasons, skies are having light to moderate clouds. Moderate to heavily clouded skies particularly during afternoons and evenings are common in the period from March to May. Due to southwest monsoon rainfall, the climate becomes very damp. There is a wide variation in temperature between the summer and winter months (fig-1.7). the districts are encircled on three sides by hills and mountains and as to open in the west such the amount of rainfall decreases from north-east and east towards the south-west. The average rainfall (fig-1.8) of the districts stands at 276 cm. Rainfall occurs nearly all year round, being the least amount in the period of November to February. From March to May the rainfall mostly occurs as thunderstorms showers and the total amount constitutes about a quarter of the annual total amount of rainfall. The southwest monsoon arrives over the districts by about the beginning of June. The rainfall in the southwest monsoon season from June to September amounts to 66 percent of the annual rainfall. July is the rainiest month. On average there are about 133 rainy days in a year. The highest maximum temperature

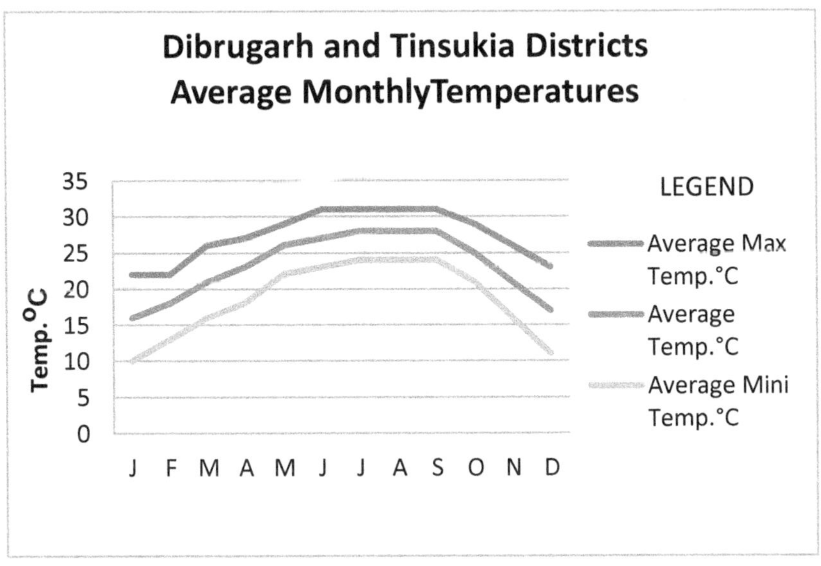

Fig-1.7

recorded at Dibrugarh was 38.9^0 c. By about the end of November, both day and night temperature decreases rapidly. January is the coldest month with the mean daily minimum temperature between 8^0 and 10^0c. In this season cold waves affect the region in the wake of the passing of westerly disturbance when the minimum temperature may go down to 5^0c or less. From about the beginning of March, the temperature begins to rise. The period from March to May continued to be pleasant constituting the pre-monsoon period.

The period from July to August constitutes the hottest period of the year with the mean daily maximum temperature at 31^0c and the mean daily minimum at 24^0c. This season is the wettest of the year.

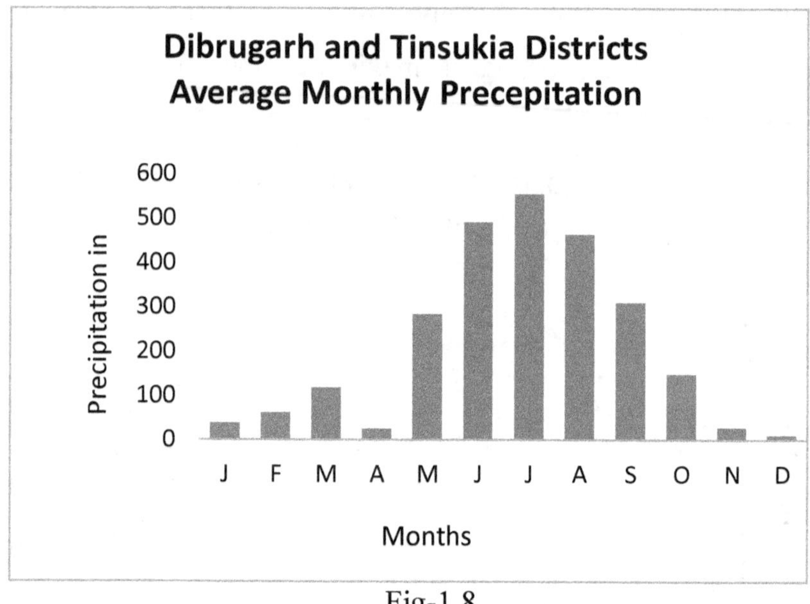

Fig-1.8

Source: Based on data from Mohanbari Airport, Dibrugarh, 2015

With the withdrawal of the southwest monsoon early in October, the weather starts becoming cooler. So, based on temporal climatic variation three seasons in a year can be distinguished in these districts. 1. Winter season-from October to February. 2. Pre-monsoon season from March to May and 3. Monsoon season- from June to September.

1. Winter Season-from October to February:- The temperature in the Dibrugarh and Tinsukia Districts starts to dip as the sun moves southward after September 23. Later in November is when winter officially starts up until the end of February, it continues.The districts experience a minimum temperature of 4°C and an average temperature of 12°C. The typical daily temperature in January, when it is the coldest, is below 10°C. The average number of foggy days per month is 28, whereas the average amount of rainfall per month during the winter is 11.8 cm.

2. Pre-monsoon Season-from March to May:-With the end of February, the temperature begins to rise in the region. March, April, and May become sufficiently hot and the rains are yet to come in their full form. Thus the pre-monsoon period is a transitional season between the dry, cool winter and the warm rainy monsoon season. The maximum average temperature during this season is 28.3°C. While the minimum comes down to 20°C.The average amount of rainfall during this season stands at 30.3 c.m. The important characteristics of this season are the rapidly increasing temperature, the disappearance of fog, and the cyclonic thunderstorm 'Bordoichila' accompanied by heavy thundershowers that occur during this season.

3. Monsoon Season- from June to September:-The season of monsoon prevails over Dibrugarh and Tinsukia Districts during June, July, August, and September. The total amount of rainfall during this period accounts for 85 percent of the annual average. July and August record high rainfall about 130 c.m. The average amount of rainfall during this season is 233.8 mm. By early June the S.W. Monsoon registers its arrival in the Assam valley with the continuous heavy rainfall experienced in these districts. The Brahmaputra stays in the spate of floods, recording a sequence of peak floods up until October, as river levels rise quickly. Peak floods like these destroy a lot of land and property by flooding areas beyond the main banks.

Natural Vegetation:-

The districts of Tinsukia and Dibrugarh are abundant in different kinds of natural plants. The districts' climate, topography, and soils have created ideal circumstances for the luxuriant expansion of natural plants. The forests in these districts can be divided into the following three groups based on the species composition.

1. Mixed deciduous, deciduous forests mixed with patches of evergreen species.

2. The grassland and evergreen forests.

3. The swamp vegetation.

Now, only the reserve woods in the districts have natural vegetation. The most common type of mixed deciduous riverine woods may be found in the Dibru and Mechaki reserves. Here, evergreen species are more prevalent in the lower canopies whereas deciduous species dominate the top canopy. This type of forest can be easily categorized into Hollock areas. The Hollock (Terminalia myriocarpa) forests occupy only a very small portion of these forests and are generally confined to flabby land where the soil is usually rich and drainage condition is also good. Among other kinds of trees mentioned may be made of uriam, (Bischofia javanica) Outenga, (Dillenia indica) Morhal, (Vatica lanceofolea) Jamuk, Thekera, etc. The majority of these mixed deciduous woods are sparsely populated and fall into the open area category, yet in other regions, dense stands of bamboo (Bambusa) and cane have made these forests nearly impenetrable.

The reserve forests of Jakai, Telpani, Namdang, and Dihingmukh are known to include semi-evergreen woods. The woodland is not very good in general.Nahar (Mesua ferrea) and Outenga (Dillenia indica) are generally seen in these forests and other associates of Nahar are Uriam, Jutuli, Outenga, Ajar, (Largerstoroemia parvilora) Hillikha (Terminalia chebula), etc. Similarly, the associates of Outenga are Uriam (Andrachne trifoliate), Morhal, Ajar (Lagerstromia flos reginae), etc. The open areas of these reserves are generally covered with grasses and weeds and some isolated trees. Patidoi is the most common undergrowth in the Outenga while Sorat (Laportia crenulate) and Dighloti are common in open areas.

Evergreen forests as the name implics are evergreen in character and cover the rest of the reserve forests starting from the Dangori and Doom Dooma reserve forests and stretching further south to the end of the district and beyond. This type occurs in the western part of the districts representing the climax vegetation of the locality with species like Hollong (Dipterocarpus macrocarpus) and Makai (Shorea assamica).On account of the constant association of Hollong (Dipterocarpus macrocarpus) with Nahar (Messua ferrea), these forests are more popularly known as Hollong Nahar forests of Upper Assam. The more important timber species of this type of forest are Amari (Amoora wallichii), Gonsoroi, Hollong, Poma (Cedrela toona), Som, Champa, etc. A very common tree of the lower canopy is Morhal, which is now extensively used for fencing posts (Govt. of India, 1976).

The majority of the soil on the river banks and riverine islands is sand. Long-term water retention is not possible with this sort of soil. Thus towering trees, except a few species such as Simul, Khoir, etc. cannot flourish in these locations. Riparian vegetation refers to the plants that grow on riverbanks and islands. The riparian vegetation in these districts is mostly tall grasses (Kher, Ikara, Khagari, etc.). Along with grasses, these areas contain Simul, Khoir, and Kadam trees. In the Brahmaputra valley, there are many marshes and swamps. These support various types of swamp grasses and other plants like Lily, Lotus, Waterwort, Water hyacinth, Taro, etc.

2 CULTURAL BASES

Regional Population and Ethnic Base:-

Population Size and Distribution:-

The Dibrugarh and Tinsukia Districts have respective populations of 26, 44, 696 as of the 2011 Census. In comparison to 2001, the population density increased to 369 people per km². Despite the state's 78,438 square kilometres remaining the same, the population density has increased to 397 per square kilometre from 340 in 2001. Dibrugarh and Tinsukia districts have comparable populations that make up 4.25% of Assam's total population.

It wasn't until the first half of the 13th century A.D. that the history of the early human occupation of Dibrugarh became known. Some accurate information was only temporally documented after the Ahom conquest of Assam in 1228 A.D. It is unclear exactly when these individuals arrived in the Dibrugarh district and began to rule there. Due to the lack of proper historical evidence, their origin is also highly controversial. The population of the district can broadly be divided into two groups. The first one is the indigenous people those who settled before the annexation of the district by the British and the second one is those who settled after annexation. The post-independence period saw a significant change in the pattern of population distribution and occupancies in the area, with the arrival of people from former East Pakistan (current Bangladesh), graziers and farmers from Nepal, defence personnel, service holders, and supporting businessmen. Dibrugarh and Tinsukia districts had very few villages in 1901, and most of those settlements were tiny hamlets with less than 500 people (Borooah,1985). The district has advanced greatly in the last few decades in terms of industry, agriculture, medical assistance, etc. More villages have developed as a result of increased human habitation, robbing nature of its wilderness. The villages with ill-defined boundaries described in early records have gradually changed into more homogenous and compact units with roads, schools, and other essential amenities for modern living.

The district's total population after its annexation by the East India Company (in 1826) was 38,829 (Pemberton,1832). In 1835, the establishment of tea gardens started in the region. The population began to increase and by 1841, it became 50,000 as per the record of Robinson (1841). The Mill's Report recorded a population of 45,175 in the region for the year 1847-48, showing a remarkable decrease from the earlier record. From 1853 onwards population of the districts began to increase at a rapid rate as a result of the immigration of tea garden labourers. In 1853, nine tea gardens were opened up in these districts and during this period (1853-1872) the population growth was 88.4 percent. The population growth of the districts had been still sharper since 1872, which recorded a 1718.59 percent increase during the century

(1872-1971) from 82,109 to 14, 11,119. The rate of growth thus, is much higher than the growth of 601.6 percent in Assam and 154.5 percent in India, during the period. The annual fluctuation, of course, is not considered in the data of the districts.

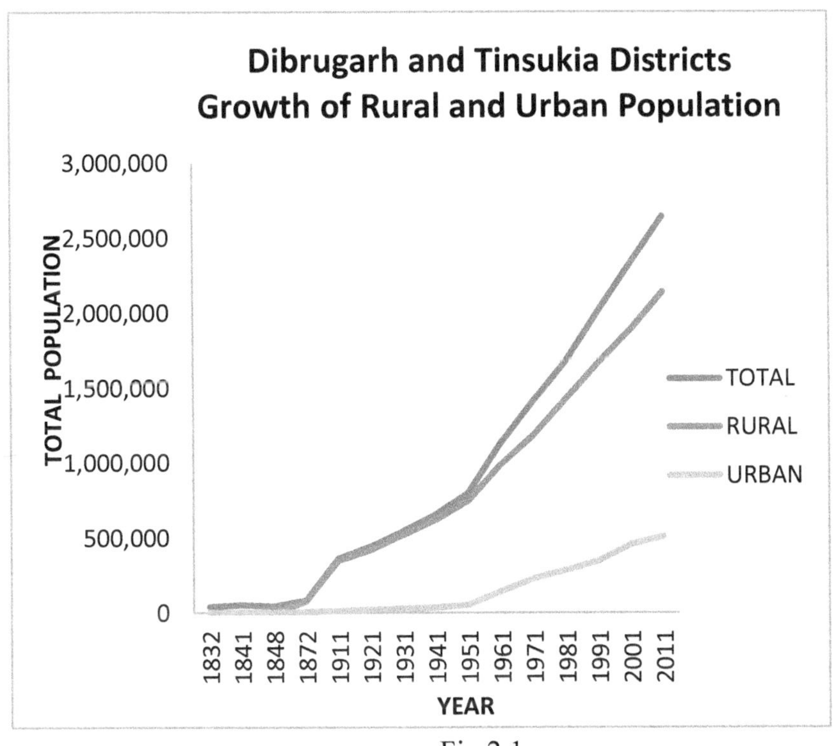

Fig-2.1

Source :(i) Hunter, (1879, Rep 1975);

(ii) Census of India 1971, 1991, 2001 series 3, Assam Part VI-A Town Directory and

iii) Allen, (1905)

It can be seen that the 1911 population density for the Dibrugarh and Tinsukia districts was 4.4 times higher than the

1872 density. In 1872–73, there were 11.5 people per square kilometre, compared to 368.8 people per square kilometre currently. 2516 settlements are currently populated as of 2011. In 2011, 13.3% of the district's entire population was made up of scheduled tribes, and 6.63 percent was made up of scheduled castes.

Between the Dangori-Dibru Rivers in the north and Burhi Dihing in the south are the districts, which are primarily lowland good for paddy farming with some somewhat highland suitable for tea. Therefore, a dense concentration of people can be seen in the tea gardens, paddy fields, villages, and towns in this area. Mineral resources and transportation and communication infrastructure are two other elements that have an impact on distribution. The population is concentrated along the highways and railroad tracks. Similarly oil and coal extraction has contributed to population concentration in Namrup, Naharkatiya, Duliajan, Digboi, Margherita, and Ledo.

The growth of the urban population in the districts is found to be very rapid after 1872 as shown in appendix-2.1. It is to be noted, however, that before 1921, Dibrugarh, the headquarters Town was the only urban center in the districts. An analysis of the process of urbanization reveals that the districts have passed through four distinct phases. The first phase (1842-1921) was a phase of slow urban growth, the second phase (1921-1951) was a period of gaining momentum of further urbanization and the third phase (1951-1971) was a period of rapid urbanization and (1971-2011) again slow down of urban growth (fig-2.2).

The urban population growth in the districts between 1872 and 1911 was low yet comparatively high. Table 2.1 shows that the growth rate during this time was 276.3%, which is significantly higher than the 21.8% growth rate in India and about 211.3% growth rate in Assam. The migration of people from different regions of Assam and India, representing a range of racial affinities, was largely responsible for this increase when the districts started to be recognised as a place with economic and industrial potential.

Dibrugarh and Tinsukia Districts
Phases of Urbanization

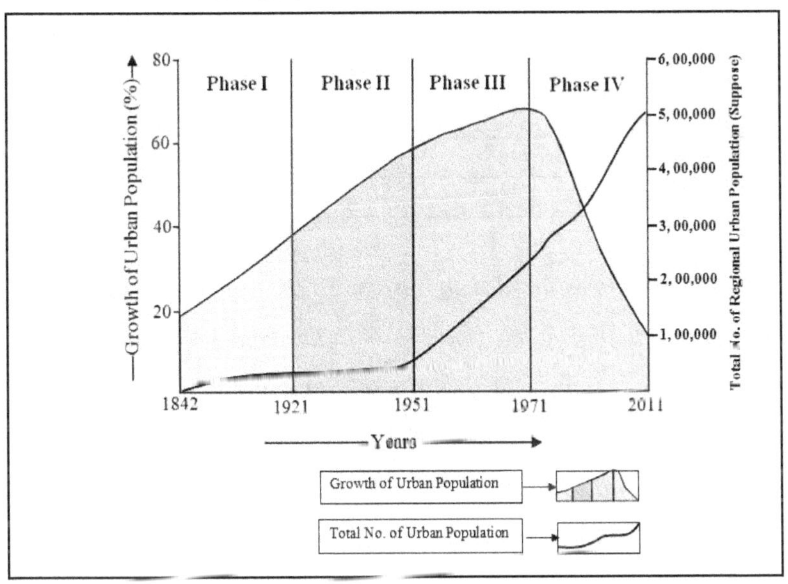

Fig-2.2

Table-2.1
Dibrugarh and Tinsukia Districts
Growth of Rural and Urban Population
Compared to Assam and India 1872-2001

Year	Total	Dibrugarh and Tinsukia Districts Region				Assam		India	
		Rural	P.C. of Growth	Urban	P.C. of Growth	Rural Growth	Urban P.C. of Growth	Rural P.C. of Growth	Urban P.C. of Growth
1872	82,109	78,239	-	3,870	-	-	-	-	-
1911	3,61,82	3,47,26	343.8	14,563	276.	83.9	211.	16.8	21.8
1921	4,39,85	4,19,60	20.8	20,249	39.0	20.0	36.8	1.29	8.27
1931	5,43,76	5,17,97	23.4	25,744	27.4	19.7	27.5	9.98	19.1
1941	6,56,22	6,22,51	20.2	33,706	30.4	20.1	28.3	11.8	31.9
1951	7,98,73	7,45,40	19.7	53,336	58.3	18.4	65.7	8.79	41.4
1961	11,26,4	9,84,87	32.1	1,41,57	165.	30.8	126.	20.6	26.4
1971	14,11,1	11,83,5	20.2	2,27,53	60.7	32.6	65.0	21.8	38.2
1981*	16,75,0	14,23,0	18.01	2,84,89	22.2	21.9	38.2	19.3	46.1
1991	20,04,7	16,62,5	19.03	3,42,25	23.0	22.5	39.5	20.0	36.4
2001	23,25,1	18,82,7	13.25	4,52,39	32.1	16.5	38.2	18.1	31.5
2011	26,44,6	21,37,9	13.55	5,06,75	12.0	15.3	27.6	12.1	31.8

There was no census in 1981 in Assam. So the population figure for 1981 of Assam, Dibrugarh, and Tinsukia Districts are as per Govt. office estimated records, Directorate of Statistics.

Source :(i) Hunter, (1879, Rep 1975);

(ii) Census of India 1971, 1991, 2001 series 3, Assam Part VI-A Town Directory and

(iii) Allen (1905)

Ethnic Structure of Population and Process of Peopling:-

The Assam or Kamrupa region previously belonged to a kingdom called Pragjyotishpura, and its inhabitants were known as Kiratos, according to Hindu mythological scriptures including the Mahabharata and Puranas. The Kiratos who lived in the study districts belonged to the monarchy as well. The huge Bodo group of the Tibeto Chinese family included the "Kiratos," a race of Mongoloid ancestry. The first known settlers of the area include the modern-day Bodos, Kacharis, Chutiyas, Deoris, and Mishings. (Chatterjee, 1974)

The Dibrugarh and Tinsukia regions are home to the indigenous Bodo people (table-2.2). They had settled in the area long before the Christian era came into being. The study then turned into territory beneath the Chutiyas' region. It was thereafter conquered by the Ahoms king and eventually by the Britishers. The Ahoms are thought to have arrived in these areas before any other Tai-Shan immigrants. Several Tai-Shan communities, including Phakials, Khamtis, various Bodo groups, Mishings, and Singphos began to settle in the Dibrugarh and Tinsukia districts during their rule. Thus the process of peopling over these districts is a continuous process and is still going on. Throughout history, there have been ups and downs in the tendency to populate. People were sometimes forced to leave certain regions, while other times they had the opportunity to resettle the districts, due to frequent and recurrent barbarous conflicts, natural calamities like earthquakes, floods, and diseases, as well as administrative compulsions. One of Assam's earliest native populations is the Kacharis (Bodo and others). The earliest settlers in these districts were the Kacharis. They inhabited the areas west of the river Disang and south of the Brahmaputra and were known by many names in various locations and at various times throughout the entirety of north-eastern India of the Indian subcontinent. However, the Ahoms significantly increased their dominance in the sixteenth century, and they drove the Kacharis from their capital east of the Dikhow River.

The Chutiyas are one of the plain tribes in the district, along with the Kochs and the Ahoms. They also belong to the Bodo family, along with the Garo, Kachari, and Tipperary. It is believed that their first home was among the hills in the Subansiri river basin. This group consists of the subgroups of Hindu, Ahom, Deori, Miri, and Borahis, who live in the Dibrugarh and Tinsukia areas.

Another branch of the Bodo group that belongs to the Tibeto-Burman language subfamily is the Moran and Motoks. Mongkong in the Hukong valley of the upper Chindwin River is where the Morans first lived. They are presently restricted to the districts of Tinsukia and Dibrugarh. Medieval settlers Mishing, Singpho, and Duonias belonged to the Tibeto-Burman branch of the Mongloid race. In the hills of what is now Arunachal Pradesh, the Mishings were first settled in the upper reaches of the Subansiri

River. The Adis of Arunachal Pradesh is similar to the Mishing in terms of language. Singphos belonged to the Tibeto-Burman Kachin group, who migrated in the later medieval period around 1793 A.D. from the Irrawaddy river bank and started to dwell on the Tengapani river bank south of the Lohit river and the bank of the Burhi-Dihing river.

Table -2.2
Dibrugarh and Tinsukia Districts
Origin and Peopling of Human Groups in Different Periods

Periods	People groups	Subgroups
Post Independence	Indo-Aryan	(i) Bengali & Hindustani-all Both Hindus and Muslims (ii) Rajasthanis (Hindus) (iii) Nepalis (Hindus) (iv) Others(Hindus, Muslims, and Christians)
British	(1) Austro-Asiatic- (2)Tibeto-Chinese- (3) Indo-Aryan-	-Proto-Australoid and Mundari descent -Siamese Chinese-Kuki-chin, Kachin, Meitei -All medieval groups, Rajasthani, Nepalis, North Indian Hindus &Muslims, Bengali Muslims.
Medieval	(1)Mongoloid (i) Tibeto-Chinese- (ii)Tibeto-Burman- (2) Indo Aryan	(i) Siamese-chinese Tai group, Phakial, Khamti, Khamyang, Aitonia, Turung, (ii) Siamese-Chinese Tai-shan group-Ahoms. Mishings, Singpho(Kachin group), Duonia (mixed) Assamese caste Hindus, Assamese Muslims, Bengali.
Ancient	Indo Aryan	Assamese caste Hindus,

		Bengali.
Proto-historic	Indo Aryan Mongoloid (Tibeto-Burman)	Assamese caste Hindus, Bengali. Bodo, Kachari, Chutias, Barahis, Morans ,Motoks, Nagas
Pre-historic	Mongoloid (Tibeto-Burman) or Austro- Asiatic-	Bodo, Kachari, Chutias, Barahis, Morans ,Motoks, Nagas, Khasis (Mon-Khmer speaking) of Syntengs & Pnars.

Tabulation by Author- Source: Taher, (1987)

The Assamese who was first captured by the Singphos married them and settled in the Duonias, an area in the eastern section of the Dibrugarh district. The Duonias are now recognised as a tribe, and Margherita Thana is home to many of these tribes.

Early medieval Assamese settlers of the Tai-Shan group, a Siamese-Chinese subfamily known as the Ahoms, are of Mongoloid ancestry. They migrated from upper Burma and started a settlement in Assam around 1228 A.D. and settled in the Dibrugarh district occupying the land by pushing some of the older settlers like Borahis, Morans, Chutiyas, etc. The Ahoms were brought under direct subjugation after crossing into Assam through the Patkai range in the southeast of the Dibrugarh and Tinsukia Districts, and they forged peace treaties with the Nagas, Deuri-Chutiyas, Mishmis, Singphos, and other peoples who lived close to the Ahom kingdom's border.

The late medieval Tai-Shan group of immigrants and settlers are known as Phakials, Khamtis, and Khamyangs. Phakials were originally from the Mongkong region of upper Burma, arriving in Assam in about 1760 A.D. At Margherita Thana, they chose to dwell along the Burhi Dihing river's banks. In the 18th century, Khamyang also moved from Mongkong to the Margherita region. Then, Khamtis also arrived in Assam from the Myanmar side of the Irrawaddy river.

The castes that made up the medieval Indo-Aryan settlers were Brahmins, Ganaks, Kayasthas, Kalitas, and Koches. They are related racially to the high castes of North India, claims Hutton. Nonetheless, the majority of them stayed restricted to the Brahmaputra valley's lower reaches. A limited number of caste Hindu communities arrived in the Dibrugarh and Tinsukia Districts during the 13th century A.D. and stayed there.

Since the start of the 20th century, several Muslims have also lived in the region. Tea garden labourers have settled in the Dibrugarh and Tinsukia Districts because of the expansion in tea hectares, particularly following the British occupation of Assam. They are Austro-Asiatic and Dravidian-speaking tribal people from the Santhal, Munda, Savara, and Gond people groups. They were brought by the British from the Chotanagpur plateaus to engage them in the tea plantations. These laboures have permanently settled in the region and identify themselves now as the local inhabitants. The new settlers of Indo-Aryan stock came after the

Independence of India as such the studied region has been spotted by different language-speaking people like Assamese, Bengali, Bihari, Rajasthani, etc. Thus among the new settlers, there are service holders, traders, businessmen, etc. Most of the people who come newly engaged themselves as Barbers, washermen, watchmen, sweepers, carters, porters, etc. There are a lot of immigrants from Nepal living in the Districts, and they work as graziers and farmers as well as watchmen, police officers, and semi-skilled technicians in the mining and urban centres (Borooah,1985). In addition to the aforementioned smaller ethnic groups, these districts also saw the settlement of Chinese, Anglo-Indians, Tamils, Telegus, and Malayalees. Therefore, a diverse population has developed throughout time in the Dibrugarh and Tinsukia Districts.

Occupational Pattern:-

The majority of the working population in 1872 consisted of peasants who were largely engaged in the cultivation of rice and labourers who worked on tea plantations. Traditional subsistence farming was favoured by Native People over all other forms of employment. In addition to subsistence agriculture and tea plantations, there was a modest amount of trade and commercial activity, some manufacturing—primarily the creation of earthen pots and cotton textiles—as well as coal mining and MUGA, both of which had a significant local impact.

The district's occupational structure changed by 1901. At this time, plantations, mining, manufacturing, construction, trade and commerce, transport and communication, storage, and other services rapidly supplanted the subsistence peasant economy that had predominated in the preceding century. In contrast to the rise of plantation workers from 11.6 percent to 47.2 percent of the working population during the same period, the percentage of the working population engaged in agriculture decreased from 88.4 percent in 1872 to 52.8 percent by 1901.

Compared to the state's 9.7 and the nation's 8.7, the Dibrugarh district had a working population percentage of up to 12.0 in other services. The employees of government, semi-government, and private organisations, who were primarily based in the Dibrugarh and Tinsukia sub-divisional headquarters, are among the other services. There were roughly 6,000 government workers in 1971. Besides, there were a considerable number of people working in private firms also.

Literacy and Cultural Base: -

In 2001, the literacy rate in the districts of Dibrugarh and Tinsukia was 64.95 percent. Rural and urban areas had literacy rates of 59.53 and 86.06 percent, respectively. Women make up 55.37 percent of literature as a whole. Scheduled castes and tribes had literacy rates of 79.72 percent and 73.98 percent, respectively. The literacy rate was 64.42 percent in 2011, showing a little decline from the preceding few years. The large influx of illiterate people, the lack of infrastructure to support a population that is suddenly growing, and the emergence of economic issues that discourage children from attending school could all be contributing factors to the drop in literacy rates in the Dibrugarh and Tinsukia Districts.

The Ahom period witnessed notable literary and artistic advancement in Assamese literature, but with the arrival of the British, an effort was made to impose modern education on Assam. The first English school was founded in Dibrugarh in 1840, marking the beginning of modern education in the Dibrugarh and Tinsukia areas. There were only six schools in the district in 1853, and the rolls held 170 students. The advancement of education over the ensuing eleven years was characterised as being extremely slow. The entire educational system underwent a significant transformation during the following decade, 1864–1874. Both the number of schools and the number of students roughly ten-fold rose. In the entire Dibrugarh and Tinsukia Districts, there are 2027 primary, 587 middles, 342 high, 44 higher secondary, and 12 junior colleges as of September 30, 2007.

Geopolitical Base:-

When the Ahoms first arrived in Assam in the early thirteenth century, the Chutiyas controlled the area of the Dibrugarh and Tinsukia Districts to the east of the Burhi Dihiing River. By defeating the Chutiyas in the north and the Kacharis in the south, the Ahoms rose to become the dominant force in the Brahmaputra Valley and expanded their dominion in Assam. Before the British arrived, the current Dibrugarh and Tinsukia Districts' jurisdiction saw the rise to power of Moamarias, Khamis, and Singphos.

The Governor-General in Council proclaimed in 1839 annexing his land to Bengal, separating it into the districts of Sibsagar and Lakhimpur and ordered that these two districts be managed similarly to the other districts of lower Assam.

Lakhimpur, which comprises Matak and Sadiya and both the northern and southern reaches of the Brahmaputra, was governed using the same system as the rest of Assam proper until the Panchayat courts were created in August 1842. It is clear that until 1842, North Lakhimpur served as the district headquarters. But, when Matak and Sadiya were added to the district, the district headquarters were moved to Dibrugarh for administrative reasons. From that year until the district's division in October 1971, Dibrugarh served as the Lakhimpur district's district headquarters. In 1873 an Inner-line had been maintained on its three sides i.e north-east, east, and south-east, which served as the administrative boundary between the Dibrugarh Sub-Division and the Frontier tracts of Abor, Mishimi, and Singphos respectively. But in 1964, the Inner Line was thrown back to Tirap in the South-East, as a result of which a few of the lower hills were included in this district, enlarging the Thana of Margherita, formed in 1891. Before it, the then sub-division of Dibrugarh became the present Dibrugarh and Tinsukia Districts have consisted of only four Thanas — Dibrugarh in the west, Jaipur in the South, Doom Dooma in the east and Sadiya in the north.

Two new Thanas Tinsukia and Moran were born in the year 1911. Due to the addition of a 215 square km region to the Lakhimpur Border Tract in 1914, the district saw some population growth. The Thana of Digboi first appeared in 1931. The Thana of Bordubi was established in 1941, and the same year, the Tirap Frontier Tract was created, adding a piece to the Sadiya Frontier Tract and leaving 266.8 km2 to the district.

The area that makes up the present Sadiya Thana is made up of the 414.4 square kilometre Sadiya Border Tract and the 1014.5 square kilometre foothills of the Mishimi Hills, both of which were given to the former Dibrugarh District in 1951. The Dhemaji Sub-Division was created in 1970 and contains a few areas both south and north of the Brahmaputra.

The years 1971 to 1981 saw significant developments in the Lakhimpur District. On October 2, 1971, it was divided into two districts: Lakhimpur, with its administrative centre in North Lakhimpur, and Dibrugarh, with its administrative centre in Dibrugarh. The former District of Lakhimpur's subdivision of Dibrugarh was combined to form the new district of Dibrugarh. Tinsukia Sub-Division was subsequently established, with Tinsukia serving as its headquarters.

It was decided to create the Dibrugarh subdivision, which has its headquarters there. By dividing the existing Sub-Division of Tinsukia's Sadiya Police Station, a new sub-division known as Sadiya Sub-division was created, with its headquarters in Chapakhowa.

On August 29, 1989, Tinsukia was divided from the Dibrugarh District to become a distinct district. The subdivisions of Tinsukia, Sadiya, and Margherita were combined to form the new district of Tinsukia, which has a total area of 3790 sq km. Dibrugarh and Tinsukia Districts are united and considered as one region in the study since the two districts, though administratively different, still function as a microgeographic units.

3 ECONOMIC BASES

Currently, only the tea industry employs a considerable labour force in the Dibrugarh and Tinsukia Districts, along with coal and petroleum. All other industries can be categorized as cottage and small-scale, but none of them can be regarded as a manufacturing industry in the districts' conventional definition.

Natural Resources:-

Coal: Two distinct fields located near the southern border of the Dibrugarh and Tinsukia Districts contain sizable lignite coal resources.

1) Makum Coalfield:- One of the significant and well-established coalfields close to Margherita is Makum. Between the Dirak River on the west and the Tirap River on the east is a field that is 30 km long and roughly 5 km wide. At the base, 200 m of the Tikak Parbat stage are five well-developed coal seams that are progressively 21.0 m, 2.3 m, 6.0 m, 1.6 m, and 2.1 m thick. The Makum coalfield has 249.65 million tonnes of total reserves, according to the 2000 geological survey. The two opposing branches of the Namdang syncline's eastward-sloping Namdang syncline are where the coal seams leave Namdang. The south limb of the syncline is obscured, at places, by the Haflong-Disang thrust and consequently, the coal seams extending along this limb are either highly distorted or cut off at intervals.

2) The Jaipur Coalfield:- The Jaipur coalfield spans a region that is 15 km long and around 1 km wide, located between the Buri-Dihing and the Disang rivers along the base of the Jaipur hills. Over the Disang river and into the Sibsagar area, the belt is likewise spreading further west. Within a 300-meter-thick horizon of the Tikak Parbat stage that runs along the south limb, this area has several coal seams, at least five of which have been proven to be viable. The main one is up to 6.5 m. thick while the others are various in thickness between 0.9, and 2.0 m. the richest development of the seams is in the vicinity of the Disang river where M/S Joypore Colliery Limited is mining since 1954. Inferred workable reserves of coal in the Jaipur field, up to a depth of 300m, will be about 54.02 million tonnes (Geological survey, 1995). The production was nearly 2,866 tonnes while it was sheet down for an indefinite period till date.

Petroleum:- The Digboi crude oil has a basis of mixed asphalt and paraffin with a small number of cyclic hydrocarbons. At Digboi, crude oil is found in around 20 oil sand beds that are spaced out over a stratigraphic thickness of 1,200 metres in the Tipam sandstones of the Digboi anticline. With a total production of 0.50 million metric tonnes of crude oil up till 1953, Digboi was the sole oil-producing region in India. Nowadays, the field produces about 0.65 million metric tonnes of oil annually.

1) The Nahrkatiya Oilfield:- North of the Naga thrust, close to Jaipur, beneath a 1,500-meter-thick blanket of alluvium from the

Dihing Series, lies the Naharkatiya oil field. Between 1925 and 1938, the Assam Oil Corporation used geophysical methods of gravity prospecting to find this resource. The business began drilling in the area in 1952, and in 1953 the first test well that had been dug to a depth of 3570 metres proved to be a reliable oil producer.

2) Moran Oilfield:- Five primary oil sand horizons in the Barails contain oil in this field. The field's structure is E-W trending, with a moderate anticline fold that is divided by several faults that create useful structural traps. The Moran oil field was discovered across the western border of this district in 1956 when the first test well drilling at Moranhat encountered oil in the Barail series inside a depth of 4184 metres. This was the culmination of extensive geophysical investigations conducted by the Assam Oil business. Currently, it is projected that these two new fields will produce roughly 3,000 tonnes of goods annually.

Natural Gas:- The Naharkatiya and Moran fields include significant natural gas deposits with oil. The Assam State Electricity Board has completed a thermal power project to use this gas, and the Fertilizer Corporation of India has built a fertiliser factory. A large-scale project to build a gas-based cracker plant (BPCL) in Assam is now under development in Lapetkata, close to Dibrugarh. There is a considerable amount of natural gas production. LPG produced an annual total of 50.000 tonnes in 2008.

Agricultural Resources:-

Paddy is the major food crop of the Dibrugarh and Tinsukia districts and is produced abundantly all across the plain portions of the districts. The three types of rice that are most frequently grown in the districts are sali, 'ahu,' and 'bao,' with sali paddy producing the most. The production of high-yielding varieties of paddy has progressively gained popularity. According to the government of Assam's final projection, which was included in the "Basic Agricultural Statistics" for the 2007–2008 fiscal year, 4,855, 66,635, and 72 hectares, respectively, were planted with high-yielding varieties of autumnal, winter, and summer paddy. Other crops grown in the districts are wheat, maize, rape and mustard seeds, pulse, etc. but the total production of these items is much less than their requirements in the districts. Pulses are mainly grown in alluvial flatlands on the river banks and commonly grown pulses are Mati-Mah (Phaseolus Mungo), Magu-Mah (Phaseolus aureus), Arhar (Cajanus cojan), Masur-Mah (Lens Esenlenta), and Mator-Mah (Prisum Sativum). The cultivation of fiber crops is very limited. Throughout the districts, only cotton and jute are farmed, and only in very limited quantities. The data on the final projection of the areas under cultivation of some of the crops farmed in the area and their productions as provided in the "Basic Agricultural Statistics" for the years 2000-2001 of the Government of Assam are shown in the table below (table-3.1).

Table-3.1
Dibrugarh and Tinsukia Districts
Area, Production, and Productivity of Major Crops 2000-2001

Commodity		Area (ha)	Production(MT)	Productivity (average yield in per hectare)
Paddy	Autumn Paddy	3258	5.41	16.60
	Winter Paddy	74124	137129.00	18.50
	Summer Paddy	80	164.00	20.50
	Total	**77462**	**142701.00**	**55.60**
Wheat		85	107.00	12.60
Kharif Pulses	Arahar	185	141.00	7.60
	Black Gram	435	192.00	4.41
	Green Gram	42	19.00	4.40
	Total	**662**	**352.00**	**29.01**
Rabi	Gram	8	3.50	4.60
Pulses	Green Gram	115	49.50	4.30
	Black Gram	1160	560.30	4.80
	Pea	1450	496.00	3.40
	Total	**2725**	**1105.80**	**17.10**
Kharif oil seed	Sessamum	28	14.40	5.10
Rabi Oil Seed	Mustard	8873	5732.00	6.50
	Sessamum	155	80.60	5.20
	Ground Nut	5	3.60	7.20
	Total	**9033**	**5813.20**	**24.00**
Kharif	Vegetables	2088	14302.00	68.50
Rabi	Vegetables	3824	28450.00	74.40
	Maize	265	142.00	5.30
Fruit Crop	Banana	1686	3024.70	17.90
	Pineapple	336	477.50	14.20
	Papaya	134	202.10	15.10
	Assam Lemon	157	87.00	5.50
	Areca Nut	2756	4134.00	15.00
	Coconut	180	360.00	2.00
	Orange	250	338.00	13.50
Tuber Crops	Potato	2500	1538.00	6.15
	Sweet Potato	55	12.00	2.19
	Tapioca	10	4.10	4.09
Spices	Chillies	280	19.50	0.69
	Turmeric	450	12600.00	280.00
	Ginger	307	3684.00	120.00

Orange can be regarded as the primary fruit crop in the area and is grown in several areas of the district. Mango, Jack fruit, lichee, Assam lemon, and other fruit-bearing trees are highly prevalent in the area. Several of these trees are usually grown in practically every farmer's home.

Land Resources:-

The land in its spatial sense covers a large area apart from agricultural uses. The landholding pattern and the total land area of the Dibrugarh and Tinsukia districts are shown under the following heading (table-3.2)

Table-3.2
Dibrugarh and Tinsukia Districts
Area of Operational Holding,
Average Size of Holding, and Land use Categories

Land Holding & Average Size of holding		Dibrugarh	Tinsukia
Individual Holdings	Number	84704	103642
	Area (Hectare)	11593185	149839.95
	Average Size of holding	1.37	1.45
Joint Holdings	Number	1903	207
	Area (Hectare)	365646	1779.36
	The average size of the Holding	1.92	8.60
Institutional Holdings	Number	390	183
	Area (hectare)	34889.84	27482.22
	The average size of the Holding	89.46	150.18
Total Holdings	Number	86997	104032
	Area (Hectare)	154478.15	179101.53
	Average Size of Holding	1.78	1.72

Land Holding As per Size Class		Dibrugarh	Tinsukia
Marginal Holdings (0.50-1.00)	Number	46044	57417
	Area (Hectare)	21793.25	32870.52
Small Holdings (1.00-2.00)	Number	21531	26401
	Area (Hectare)	28867.60	36226.08
Semi Medium Holdings (2.00-4.00)	Number	14805	15458
	Area (Hectare)	40113.46	45345.62
Medium Holdings (4.00-10.00)	Number	4076	4195
	Area (Hectare)	21491.63	23983.75
Large Holdings (10.00 & above)	Number	541	561
	Area (Hectare)	42212.21	40675.56
All Size	Number	86997	104032
	Area (Hectare)	154478.15	179101.53

Total Land Area		Dibrugarh	Tinsukia
Total Geographical Area according to	Professional Survey	338100	379000
	Village Papers (Reported area)	338782	379000
	Forest	28630	134552
Not available for cultivation	Area put to non-Agricultural Uses	123166	74289
	Barren and Uncultivable Land	13548	36807
	Total	136714	111096
Other Uncultivated lands excluding fallow land	Permanent pastures & another grazing land	6170	3560
	Land under Misc, trees groves not included in net area sown	173368	20616
	Cultivable Wasteland	7126	1586
	Total	3064	25762

Fallow land	Fallow land other than the current fallow	1432	1159
	Current Fallow	5844	6757
	Total	7276	7916
	Net area sawn	135498	99674
	Total cropped area	176136	142439
	The area is sown more than once	40638	42765

Source: *Agriculture Department, Dibrugarh.*

Industrial Activities and Industries:-

Due to their abundance of natural resources, the Dibrugarh and Tinsukia Districts have grown to be Assam's most industrialised area. Petroleum, coal, plantations, and forests are the main sources of revenue for the districts' industries. The districts had the largest number of large and medium industries in Assam as of 31st December 2008. The districts recorded 879 such industries having on their fold about 38,424 employees, while 935 were obtained in the case of the Kamrup district region. The total no of small-scale industries registered under the Directorate of Industry was 221 employing about 1,642 persons in 2008. A short account of some of the important industries of the districts is given below

Petroleum-Based Industry:-

The oil region is known as Upper Assam. Five oil refineries—one each in Digboi, Guwahati, Bongaigaon, Numaligarh (all in Assam), and Barauni—are fed by the oil found in this region (Bihar). In the year 1828, the presence of petroleum in this region became acknowledged for the first time. On March 26, 1867, a successful oil strike was made at Makum. It should be noted that this was the first oil well extraction that was completed. The first oil was produced at Digboi drilling in 1889–1890, which was the beginning of India's oil industry. In December 1901, Digboi's oil refinery, the nation's first of its kind, began operating. The district's most significant oil field was found in Naharkatiya, where the first oil well was dug in May 1952. About 40 kilometres northwest of Naharkatiya, near Moran, is another significant oil region.

All of the oil wells in the Naharkatiya and Moran areas are owned by Oil India (Private) Limited, which represents a remarkable example of a public-private partnership and gives the country's industrial policy a fresh perspective. Oil India has built an 1152 km long pipeline to deliver crude oil to refineries in Guwahati and Barauni (400kms up to Guwahati)

Natural Gas-Based Industries:-

On April 2, 1971, the Assam Gas Company in Duliajan, an enterprise of the State Government, began operations. It was established to provide natural gas to different sectors and to serve as a foundation for potential petrochemical companies. The gas supplied by the endeavour serves as the fuel for the thermal power project developed in Namrup. The Assam Gas Company supplies the fertiliser factory at Namrup, which was built by the Fertilizers Corporation of India and is currently known as the Brahmaputra Fertilizer Corporation of India. The company also provides gas to numerous tea gardens for the operation of factories and related tasks.

Petro-Chemical Industry:-

The Assam Petrochemical Company, based in Namrup, officially opened its doors on June 25, 1976. Natural gas, urea, and carbon dioxide are the project's principal raw resources. Methanal Formalin and Petrolite are produced by this company. The Assam Gas Company provides natural gas, and the Namrup Fertilizer Factory produces urea and carbon dioxide.

Fertilizer Industry:-

The sole Fertilizer Corporation of India factory where natural gas is used as a raw material is the Fertilizer Plant at Namrup. The plant's first phase began operating on January 1, 1969, and its second phase on January 10, 1976. The facility is set up to make urea, sulphuric acid, and ammonium sulphate. The facility is notable for being the first where the Fertilizer Company of India handled significant erection work involving a significant percentage of machinery and equipment. The Assam Gas Company provides the gas, and the State Trade Corporation imports sulphur, the other basic element.

Coal Industries:-

Although coal was found here in 1876, it wasn't successfully exploited until the Assam Railway and Trade Company was established in 1881. Under the active management of the Assam Railway and Trade Company, collieries were gradually established in this area; all of them are located in the Thana of Margherita. In the vicinity of Makum, there are working collieries at Borgolai, Ledo, Namdang, Tikok Parbat, and Tipong.

Manufacturing and other Industries-:

Railway Workshop and other Industries:-

The Railway workshop located in Dibrugarh in Dibrugarh and Tinsukia Districts is more than a century old and is considered to be one of the largest workshops in North-East India. Besides overhauling and repairing locomotives and coaches, also manufactures a variety of the necessary parts for these. Many industries engaged in the manufacture of machinery, machine tools, and parts of steel furniture, steel structures, and various other metal products are established in the districts and the majority of these industries have come up near Tinsukia Town. The lone timber treatment and seasoning plant have been established by the Govt. Forest Department at Makum. Erstwhile plywood industries (private) at Tinsukia, Margherita, etc. had a considerable impact on industrialization and urbanization. The district has also a large number of sawmills, food processing, and brick-making industries, besides various other small-scale industries.

Plantation and Related Industries:-

Tea Cultivation and Industries:-

The terrain and soil of the Dibrugarh and Tinsukia Districts are often acidic. As the river periodically floods the area, new alluvial soils are created that are less acidic and have a higher percentage of fine sand and silt. They are organic, even alkaline soils. Acidic alluvial soils with good phosphorus content can be found in an old alluvium area close to the hills, making it ideal for growing fruit and tea. On the other hand, lowland locations with heavy clays and high nitrogen percentages produce superior rice yields. Tea can grow well in areas with year-round high humidity levels and lots of rain. As a result, tea is widely grown throughout the districts.

The most significant plantation crop in the districts is tea, which is significant to the local economy. It is the top earner of foreign exchange and only occupies land next to rice. The state's largest tea production that year was produced in an area of 1,22,514 hectares, which is the entire area under tea cultivation in the districts as of March 2007. The region has the second-best production in the state, averaging 1,839 kg per hectare.

Assam earns the unique distinction of being the highest tea-producing centre in the country. An overwhelming major proportion of the total production of tea in the country is contributed by about 770 tea gardens in the state bringing about 1,99,440 hectares of land under tea cultivation (as of 31-03-80). It is a major foreign exchange earner for the country and plays a dominant role in the economy of the state. The East India Company first became aware of the native tea plants growing in the Assam plains and hills and in northeast India in 1826, which is when the Assam tea business began to take shape. With 25,478 total tea estates in the Dibrugarh and Tinsukia districts, which produced roughly 211,376,000 kg of tea in 2005, this is a proud privilege.

Transport and Communication:-

The four modes of transport—road, train, river, and air—connect the districts of Dibrugarh and Tinsukia to the rest of the state. National Highways Nos. 37 and 38 serve as the primary thoroughfare for road connection in the region. These two motorways are connected by a network of blacktopped and earthen gravel roads that make up the road system. National Highway No.37 which was formerly known as the Assam South Trunk Road, enters the districts from Sibsagar and runs from Moran in the north-eastern direction up to Dibrugarh and then stretches along the railway line up to Doom Dooma and then further eastward to Saikhowa-ghat which stands on the bank of the river Luhit. The

Makum Lekhapani Road now known as the National Highway No-38 takes off from Makum and reaches Ledo through Digboi and Margherita. Under the public works department, provisional road lengths within the district in the category of State Highway, District roadway, and others are 218 km, 334 km, and 2114 km respectively of which only 1771 km. are surfaced (black-topped), and the rest 895 km are unsurfaced graveled (2011-2012). In respect of the number of motor vehicles on road, the only region with about 1,78,583 vehicles in 2011-2012 comes next only to Kamrup having the highest number of motor vehicles on road in the state. The number of buses, motor cars, jeeps, taxi cabs, motorcycles, and scooters, on-road in the district as recorded in 2011-2012 is 766; 47904; 621; 2431, and 1,03,634 respectively. Opening the border by Stillwell highway with Myanmar will have a great impact on the development of the districts.

A single-tracked, metre gauge line with a total length of 196 km in the region was used to create rail communication with the rest of the nation. Virtually all the places of economic and industrial importance are connected by the railway. Rail service was only started between Chittagong and Dibrugarh in 1904. The region's tea and coal industries are responsible for the growth of rail transportation in the districts. The necessity for providing an outlet for tea and coal led to the construction of the Dibru- Sadiya Railway line, the first in Assam, by the Assam Railway and Trading Company in 1885. The line runs from Dibrugarh Steamer

Ghat through tea-producing centers viz. Lahoal, Dikom, Chabua, Panitola, and Tinsukia Jn. to Makum Jn. which is 60 km. away to the southeast of Dibrugarh. Here it divides into two branches. One line runs northeast past other tea-producing centers of the region viz, Bor Hapjan, Hansara, Doom Dooma to Talap, to a distance of 16 miles. This section was extended by another 8 miles to Saikhowa Ghat in 1910. The other mainline connected the region's coal and oil-producing districts by travelling past Tingrai, Digboi, and Powai on its way south and then east to Margherita, which is 85 kilometres from Dibrugarh. The government bought the privately owned Dibru-Sadiya Railway line in April 1945, and it is now a part of the North-East Frontier Railway.

Except for four Ferry-Ghats operated by the Inland Water Transport Company, a recent project of the State Government along the Brahmaputra to connect the North and South bank, there is currently no steamer service connecting Dibrugarh with the rest of the nation. These are Dibru-Sonari-Burisuti, Dibru-Kachari-Oriamghat, Dibru-Sissi-Machkhowa, and Sadiya-Saikhowa. There are numerous additional ferry services offered along various rivers in the district by the State Government, with maintenance and oversight falling under the Public Works Department (PWD). Lately, two significant bridges have been built. One between Dibrugarh and Dhemaji for both rail and road over the Brahmaputra and the other between Saikhowa and Sadiya for the sole road over the Lohit which will have a tremendous impetus on the development of the region.In the districts, air travel is relatively new. The introduction of regular civilian air service didn't happen until the middle of the 20th century. Fokker Friendship may land at Mohanbari Aerodrome in Dibrugarh Sub-Division, which is situated about 2 kilometres from the Dibrugarh-Tinsukia Road N.H.37 and about 16 kilometres from Dibrugarh Town. Boeing service was also made available at Chabua Airfields to give travellers the amenities they need for a few days in the middle of their trip. The airstrip is located on the Dibrugarh-Tinsukia Road and is about 26 kilometres from Dibrugarh town.

Trade and Commerce:-

As previously mentioned, the Dibrugarh and Tinsukia Districts are abundant in natural resources and have sizable coal and crude oil deposits. Numerous significant industries, including those related to petroleum, tea, manufacturing, and power, have established themselves in the area. The districts export substantial amounts of their products to other regions of the nation and even to foreign markets. The most significant export among these goods is tea, which brings in a sizable quantity of foreign currency.

Another important product produced is crude oil. To get the crude to the refineries at Guwahati (Assam) and Barauni, a pipeline is used (Bihar). The discovery of new oil resources in Naharkatiya, Hogrijan, and Moran gives rise to the possibility that more than half of India's current petroleum needs may one day come from these new oil fields, helping the nation to save a sizable sum of foreign currency. Several regions of the state as well as adjacent states receive petroleum and other products from the Digboi refinery.

Another crucial resource is coal, which is produced in Assam in the Makum coal fields to a degree of roughly 80.55%. Although the Makum coalfields produce the most coal in the state in terms of quantity, the coal itself is of lower quality. It loses significance compared to other regions of India since labour prices are higher and transportation is more challenging.

At the time it was shut down by a Supreme Court ruling, plywood was a crucial export product and had a big impact on the state's economy. The Namrup Fertilizer factory produces urea and ammonium sulphate, both of which are distributed throughout the nation. The current Dibrugarh and Tinsukia districts also include the following significant commercial hubs: Tinsukia, Dibrugarh, Digboi, Doom Dooma, Margherita, Moran, Makum, Chabua, Naharkatiya, Bordubi, Panitola, etc. In practically all of the region's commercial hubs, wholesale and retail trade coexist side by side. Nonetheless, Tinsukia and Dibrugarh, two significant towns, account for the majority of the wholesale commerce. Both consumer goods and food products are covered.

Other Services:-

The districts are home to a sizable number of institutions, offices, and service centres involved in business, manufacturing, education, health and sanitation, and a variety of other activities. Engineers, doctors, lawyers, teachers, artists, painters, lab assistants, librarians, owners, managers, cashiers, accountants, stenographers, typists, office assistants, postmen, telephone operators, salesmen, housekeepers, matrons, watchmen, etc. are just as few of the many occupations represented by these offices. 783 registered factories, or 24% of Assam's total number of factories, were present in 2007. Also, it employs 29% of all state workers.

4 DISTRIBUTION OF URBAN CENTRES

Definition of Urban Centre :

World Perspective

To identify urban centres for various purposes, a variety of criteria are used. For settlement agglomerations, several nations merely specify a minimum population size. There are numerous instances given that span all the continents: Cities (Shi) in Japan with 50,000 or more residents and 60% or more of housing units in the main built-up regions employ 60% or more of the total population (including dependents) in manufacturing trade or other urban business kinds. Alternatively, a city having urban facilities and conditions as defined by the prefectural order is considered urban. In France, Communes contain an agglomeration of more than 2,000 inhabitants living in contiguous houses more than 200 metres between houses, also communes of which the major portion of the population is part of a multi-communal agglomeration of this nature. In the Netherlands, it means "urban: municipalities with a population of 2,000 or more inhabitants, Semi-Urban: municipalities with a population of less than 2,000 but with not more than 20 percent of their economically active male population engaged in agricultural and specific residential municipalities of commuters." In the United Nations Demographic Year Book,1988 some of the samples are recorded defining the urban population covering a wide range of examples from all the continents: In Botswana, "agglomerations of 5,000 or more inhabitants where 75 percent of the economic activity is of the non-agricultural type," In Ethiopia "Localities of 2,000 or more inhabitants"; in Argentina, "populated centres with 2,000 or more inhabitants,"; in the USA, "places of 2,500 or more inhabitants and urbanized area"; in Israel, "All settlements of more than 2,000 inhabitants except those where at least one-third of the household participating in the labour force earn their living from agriculture." In the erstwhile USSR, Cities, and Urban-type localities are officially designated by each of the constituent republics, usually according to the criteria of the number of inhabitants and predominance of agricultural or non-agricultural workers and their families. "Population clusters of 1,000 or more individuals" and "certain areas of the lower population" (such as vacation spots) in Australia "if they comprise 250 or more residences, of which at least 100 are occupied" (Carter, 1995). So, it will be obvious that there is very little basis for international comparison in the reported statistics for the population ratio of urban to rural areas in different nations. In any event, absolute numbers are incredibly meaningless. In the developing world, large communities may have significant agricultural populations, whilst small settlements may have urban characteristics.

The United Nations demographic yearbooks focus on each concern separately. The yearbook first addressed the issue of providing appropriate data on the world's urban population in 1952. It concluded that "urbanity does not disappear or begin in the continuum from huge agglomerations to small clusters or scattered houses; the line between urban and rural population is inherently arbitrary" (United Nations, 1955). The primary important criterion used in the international order to distinguish between urban and rural areas is the concentration of non-agricultural activities, particularly those related to industries, trade, and commerce.

Indian Perspective:-

According to the 2011 census, towns in India that have a municipality corporation, cantonment board, or notified town area committee are those that have a population of at least 5000 people and a population density of at least 1000 people per square mile or 400 people per square kilometre. At least 75 percent of the adult male population must be working in jobs other than agriculture for it to be urban.

In India, there is difficult of defining a town by population numbers because several modifications were introduced from time to time to make the definition concrete in the census report India. Through the decades 1901-51 'town' was defined by:

1. Every municipality of whatever size;

2. All civil lines (not included within municipal limits); and.

3. Permanent habitation with a continuous collection of houses of not less than 5,000 persons.

In 1951, the above criteria remained the same but added caution for those places with a somewhat larger population than 5,000 that do not possesses urban character (as decided by the state government in some states and census superintendents in others) may not be treated as towns.

A town was considered to be one that met the following criteria: (a) a population density of at least 1000 people per square mile; (b) a population of 50,000; (c) three-fourths of the working population should be employed in non-agricultural fields; and (d) the location should have a few distinct urban features and amenities as determined by the state (Mitra, 1961).

The definition of an urban place by the 1981 census was changed to (a) a place with a municipality, corporation, or cantonment or notified town area, or. (b) a place satisfying all the following:

1. Minimum population of 5,000.

2. 75 percent male working population is non-agricultural.

3. Density of at least 1,000 persons per square mile.

Because it might have a population of fewer than 5,000 people, this idea has come off as unclear. Similar to revenue villages, many of them did not qualify as towns legally or administratively and may have had a male population of 75% working in non-agricultural occupations. In the context of India, the density is too unrealistically low; states like Kerala, West Bengal, and Bihar had average densities of more than 1000 people per square mile. In the case of India, a far higher number (about 1,000 people per square kilometre) would be more acceptable.

According to the census of India 1991, series-4 Assam part IX-A Town Directory, "Density of the urban population is obtained by dividing the total urban population in each size class by the total area of the towns in the corresponding size class." It is noticed that the density of the urban population in Assam is 3,481 persons per square kilometer. Among the towns, the highest density of 5,361 persons per square kilometer is noticed in class-II towns followed by class-III Towns with 4,092 and followed by class-I towns with 2,916. The lowest density is noticed in class-VI towns with 1,560. As the density of the urban population sharply rises greater in class-II towns than in class-I and class-III towns so also it abruptly comes down in class-III towns to class-II towns gradually decreasing from class-III to class-II towns. Moreover, class II and class III towns have densities that are higher than the state average, whereas class I and class IV to class VI towns have densities that are lower than the state average.

Status of Urbanization:-

Indian Scene:-

The second-highest population in the world was found in India (2011 census). Also, there is a sizable urban population there. Nonetheless, just 31.2 percent of the population is urban in 2011, suggesting that the urbanisation progress is continuing to be very gradual. Only a small improvement was shown, rising from 27.8% in 2001 to 31.12% in 2011. The number of urban dwellers in the country increased from 286.1 million in 2001 to 3771 million in 2011. In 2001 Goa had a 49.75 level which is the highest against the lowest in Himachal Pradesh of 9.8 percent, the reasons being the low pace of industrialization, transport links, and trade. Orissa and Bihar had also a low pace and were urbanized below the national average of 31.2 percent. This indicates that India still is not in a satisfactory position in terms of urbanization in the world and 70 percent population is living in villages. India had a 25% urbanisation rate compared to the global average of 45%. (2001). There is no disputing India's urbanisation backwardness when we contrast its status with that of Australia and New Zealand, where the level has nearly reached 85%.

Urban Status of Assam:-

Assam is one of those states in India that has traditionally been rural, with agriculture and related work constituting the majority of people's jobs. One of the least urbanised states in the nation is Assam. While the proportion of urban residents to the state's overall population in Assam climbed from only 4.29% in 1951 to 12.90% in 2001, it remained below the country's average of 27.78% for that year. According to the census of 2011 Assam, the decadal (2001-10) growth rate of urbanization at 27.61 percent is slower than the previous decade, even though the share of the urban population increased from 12.90 percent to 14.08 percent is much lower as compared to 31.16 percent of the national level of the urban population in 2011. The stark disparities in urbanisation amongst Assam's districts, with Kamrup (metro) district having 82 percent of the people living in cities compared to Baksa district's 1.28 percent, are another notable aspect. Guwahati, the state capital city, has a population of 25% urban residents and has had a quicker pace of urban expansion, mostly as a result of in-migration from parts of the state with inadequate infrastructure. Assam has an urban population of 43.88 lakhs which is 14 percent of the total population of the state. In the last census period 2001-2011, 81 new census towns have been added to the list of urban areas of Assam. In 2011 out of the total 126 census towns, there are 88 notified towns than 80 in 2001.

Guwahati is the only town in Assam's Class 1 region with a population of one lakh or more; the other six are Silchar, Dibrugarh, Jorhat, Nagaon, Tinsukia, and Tezpur. Guwahati is also the state's largest town. According to the 2011 census, Guwahati city and the surrounding urban agglomeration is home to more than 25% of the state's 43,88,756 urban residents. The size classes based on population, as defined in Assam, are shown in table 4.1 below.

Table-4.1
Status of Urban Population in Assam 2011

Size-class	The population as per definition	Total TCs and MBs
Class I	100,000<	7
Class II	50,000-1,00,000	8
Class III	20,000-50,000	24
Class IV	10,000-20,000	45
Class V	5,000-10,000	78
Class VI	<5000	27
Total		189

Source:-Provisional Population Tables vol-2 of 2011 Census

Urban Status of Dibrugarh and Tinsukia Districts:

Dibrugarh and Tinsukia Districts in Assam, where 38.4% of the state's population lives in its 22 urban centres, are the most urbanised districts, according to the 2011 Census. Compared to the Kamrup (M) district, the urban population growth rate in the districts of Dibrugarh and Tinsukia is 13.15 percent each decade. In 2001, there were 19 metropolitan centres and over 45 growth points distributed throughout the districts. At present in the 2011 census, there are four more new towns added named Kachujan Gaon, Chapakhowa town, Forest village Lakhipathar, and

Nizmankata which towns are only treated for census purposes. These are not independent towns except Chapakhowa Town where Kachujan is a part of Tinsukia Town, Lakhipather is rural and Niz Mankata is a part of Dibrugarh Town. On the other hand, Duliajan no-1 urban centre has been excluded from urban centres in the census of 2011 of Dibrugarh district. Among 22 towns 2 have Municipal boards, 6 have town committees and the remaining 10 towns are census towns treated as such for census purposes either because they fulfill the eligibility criteria or because of their predominant urban characteristics (Appendix-4.1). According to the size of the population out of 13 towns, 2 are class I, 4 are class III, 5 are class IV, and 2 are class V towns as given in table- 2.2. It is to be noted that at present there is no class II town in Dibrugarh and Tinsukia Districts as per the census.

Table 4.2
Dibrugarh and Tinsukia District
Progress of Urban Population 1901 to 2011

Nos	Urban Centre	Population/ Class	1901	1911	1921	1931	1941	1951	1961	1971	1991	2001	2011
1	Dibrugarh	P	11,217	14,563	16,007	18,734	23,191	37,991	58,480	80,345	120,127	133,571	1,45,220
		C	IV	IV	IV	IV	III	III	II	II	I	I	I
2	Chabua	P								3,888	6,104	17,433	8,788
		C								VI	V	V	V
3	Naharkatia	P								10,774	15,052	15,523	18,924
		C								IV	IV	IV	IV
4	Duliajan Oil Town	P								11,497	17,017	23,763	29,350
		C								IV	IV	III	III
5	Namrup	P								7,972	19,740	19,021	15,483
		C								V	IV	IV	IV
6	Bar Bari A.M.C. Area	P									5,540	4,090	2,879
		C									V	VI	VI
7	Sarupathar Bengali	P										6,609	8,755
		C										V	V
8	Moran Town	P										6,826	8,445
		C										V	V
9	Niz-Mankata	P											5,920
		C											V
10	Tinsukia	P			3,080	5,160	8,338	12,245	28,468	549,11	73,918	101,957	115,556
		C			VI	V	V	IV	III	II	II	I	I
11	Doomdooma	P			1,162	1,900	2,177	3,099	8,192	10,510	15,121	19,806	21,469
		C			VI	VI	VI	VI	V	IV	IV	IV	III

No	Name												
12	Digboi T.C	P							18,235	16,538	19,137	20,553	21,791
		C							IV	IV	IV	III	III
13	Digboi Oil Town	P							16,793	15,850	16,796	16,590	11,927
		C							IV	IV	IV	IV	IV
14	Makum	P								5,992	11,993	15,118	16,875
		C								V	IV	IV	IV
15	Margherita	P								9,250	21,709	24,049	26,913
		C								V	III	III	III
16	Ledo Town	P										8,571	11,718
		C										V	IV
17	Ledo Tikok	P										6,764	5,093
		C										V	V
18	Bahbari gaon	P										6,166	6,828
		C										V	V
19	Borgolai Gant NoII	P										4,383	5,240
		C										VI	V
20	Kachujan Gaon	P											3,253
		C											VI
21	Chapakhowa Town	P											10,320
		C											I V
22	Forest Vill.Lakhipathar	P											6,027
		C											V

Source: Census of India Series-3 Town Directory1991,2001,2011 (P-population, C-class)

Note: *Niz Mankata and Borbari are part of Dibrugarh Urban Centre, Digboi oil town and Digboi T.C. have no separate identity only having two-point of concentration and areas of administration. Bahbari and Kachujan are part of Tinsukia urban area. Ledo and Ledo Tikok are in the same areas; Duliajan oil Town, Duliajan No-1 and Sarupather Bengali are the same towns having two nodes, and Borgolai and forest vill Lakhipather are not at all urban. Hence parts of urban areas are combined and will be treated as a single urban centre henceforth. Some Census identification is not at all scientific and meaningful and does not serve the purpose of urban studies. Hence from table 2.2, a modified table is prepared and these combined urban centres will be treated as single urban centres in the study onwards.*

Table-4.3
Dibrugarh and Tinsukia Districts
Population of Urban Centres 1991-2011 (Modified)

	Urban Centres	1991 (Pop with class)	2001 (Pop with class)	2011 (Pop with class)
1	Dibrugarh	Dibrugarh M.B+ Barbari AMC Area1,20,127+ 5,540=1,25,667 I	Dibrugarh M.B+ Barbari AMC Area 1,33,571+4,090= 1,37,661 I	Dibrugarh M.B+Barbari AMC Area+ NizMankata 1,45,220+2,879+5,920 =1,54,019 I
2	Tinsukia	Tinsukia MB 73,918 II	Tinsukia MB +Bahbari1,01,957 + 6,166=1,08,123 I	TinsukiaMB+Bahbari I KachujanGaon1,15,556+6,828 + 3,253=1,34,392 I
3	Digboi	Digboi TC+Digboi OilTow16,796 + 19,1373= 35,933 III	Digboi TC+Digboi Oil Town 16,590+20,553 =37,143 III	Digboi TC+Digboi Oil Town 21,791+16,875=38,666 III
4	Duliajan	Duliajan Oil Town 17,017 IV	Duliajan OilTown +Duliajan No.1+ Sarupather Bengali 23,763+1,602+6609 =31,974 III	Duliajan Oil Town+ Duliajan No.1+Sarupathar Bengali 29,350+8,755 =38,105 III
5	Ledu	-	Ledu I Ledu Tikak 8,571+6,764=15,335 IV	Ledu+Ledo Tikak 11,718+5,093=16,811 IV
6	Dooom Dooma	15,121 IV	19,806 IV	21,469 III
7	Margherita	21,709 III	24,049 III	26,913 III

8	Naharkatia	15,052 IV	15,523 IV	18,924 IV
9	Namrup	19,740 IV	19,021 IV	15,483 IV
10	Makum	11,993 IV	15,118 IV	16,875 IV
11	Chabua	6,10 V	17,433 IV	8,788 V
12	Moran	-	6,826 V	8,445 V
13	Chapakho wa	-	-	10,320 IV

Source: (Census of India Series 3, Assam 1991, 2001, 2011 Town Directory) as compiled by the author

Distribution of Urban Centres

Spatial Distribution

Urban centres' spatial distribution (fig. 4.1) will produce a pattern of concentration or dispersion in the districts. The spatial distribution of rural and urban populations is depicted in fig. 4.2 below based on their absolute sizes (table-4.3). An understanding of the occupancy, concentration, or dispersion of people in a given area can be gained from the study of population distribution. The distribution of the population (1971, Thana wise and 2011, Circle wise) through time and space in the Dibrugarh and Tinsukia Districts have been shown with the help of dots and circles (fig-4.4 and fig- 4.5). The highest concentration of urban population has been observed in Dibrugarh and Tinsukia Thana/circle while the highest concentration of rural population is in Doom Dooma Thana/circle area in both the year.

DIBRUGARH AND TINSUKIA DISTRICTS
Location of Urban Centres
2013
N
95°0'0"E
95°30'0"E
96°0'0"E
28°0'0"N
27°30'0"N
27°0'0"N
SL.No. | Urban Centres
1 Dibrugarh
2 Tinsukia
3 Moran
4 Chabua
5 Makum
6 Doom Dooma
7 Chapakhowa
8 Digboi
9 Margherita
10 Ledu
11 Duliajan
12 Naharkatia
13 Namrup
LEGEND
State Boundary
District Boundry
Sub divisional Boundary
Railway
Road
NH
Urban Centres
0 10 20 40
Kilometers
Source: Google Image 2013; Dibrugarh Town & Country Planning1971.

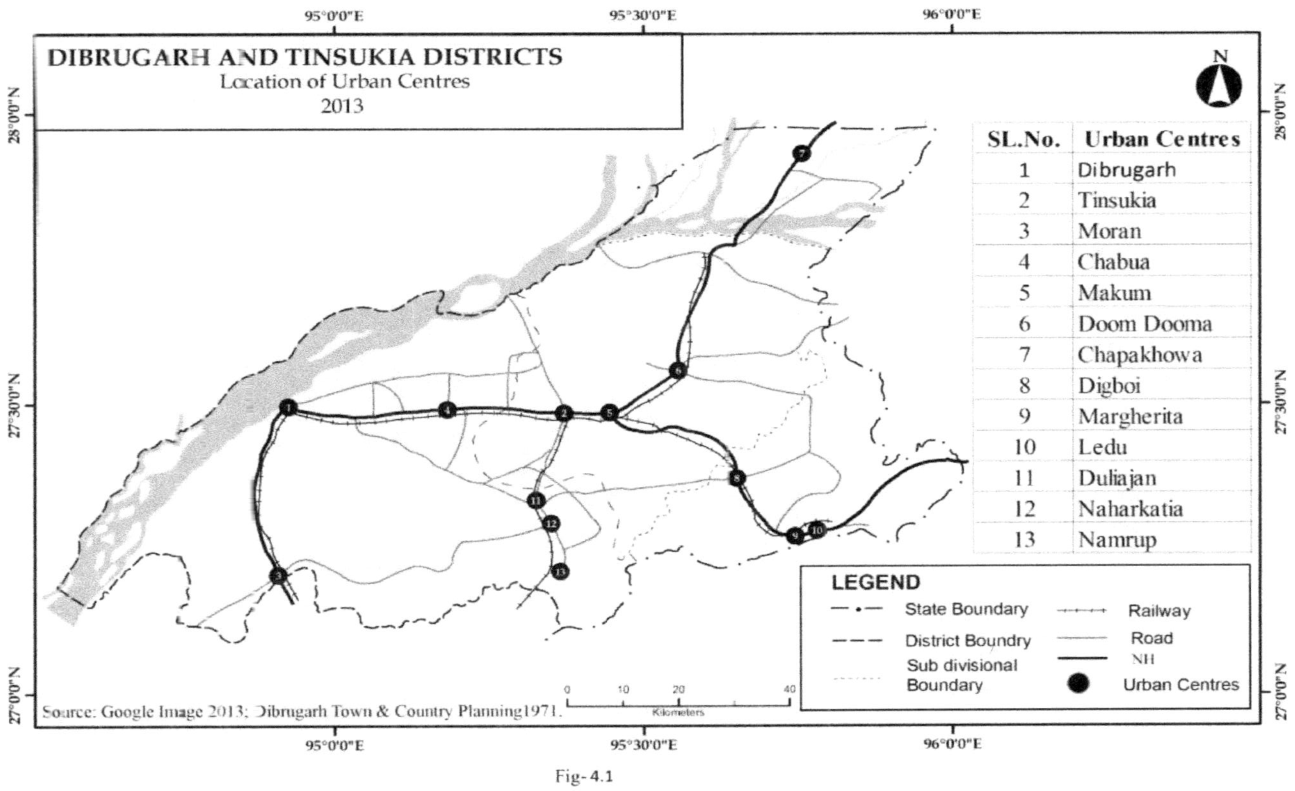

Fig- 4.1

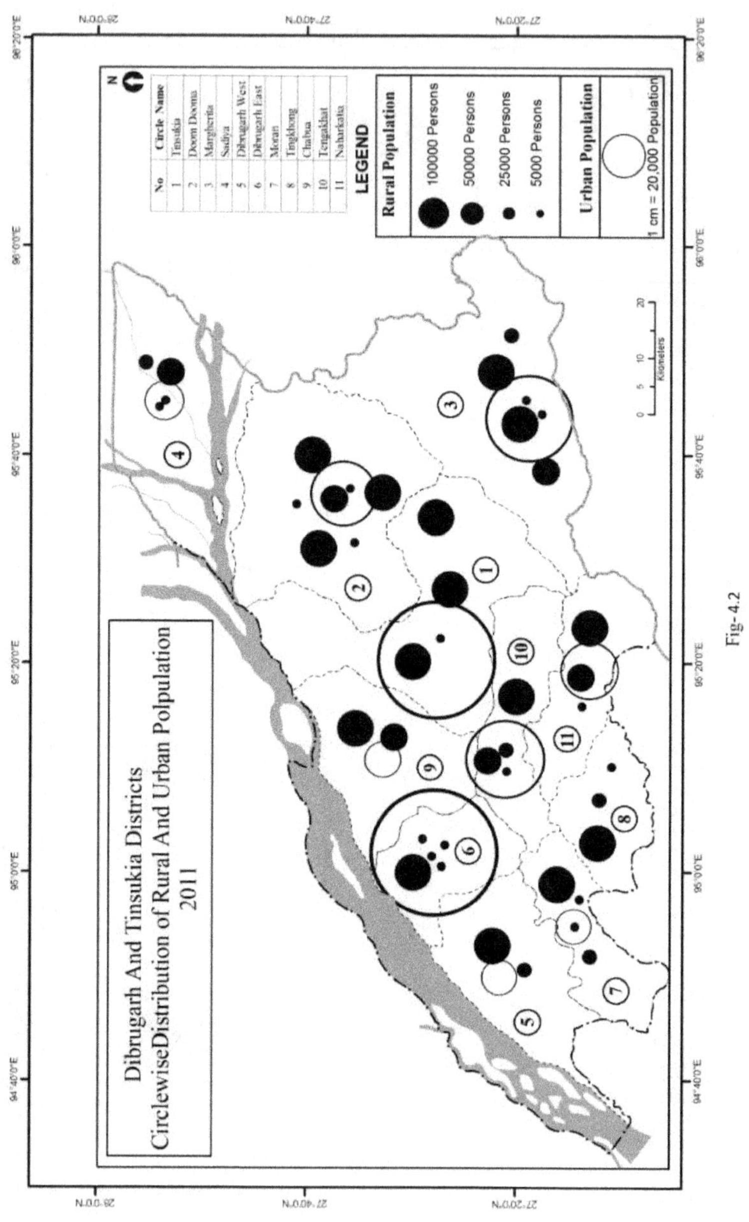
Dibrugarh And Tinsukia Districts
CirclewiseDistribution of Rural And Urban Polpulation
2011
No | Circle Name
1 | Tinsukia
2 | Doom Dooma
3 | Margherita
4 | Sadiya
5 | Dibrugarh West
6 | Dibrugarh East
7 | Moran
8 | Tingkhong
9 | Chabua
10 | Tengakhat
11 | Naharkatia
LEGEND
Rural Population
100000 Persons
50000 Persons
25000 Persons
5000 Persons
Urban Population
1 cm = 20,000 Population
Kilometers
Fig- 4.2

The ratio of people to land is expressed by the population density. By dividing the population figure by the equivalent area, it is calculated. Given the importance of two key geographical components, namely the land and the people, the density of the population assumes significantly significance. According to fig. 4.3, the population density in the Dibrugarh and Tinsukia Districts exhibits extremely distinct geographical patterns. Dibrugarh East, which was the historically occupied portion of the Dibrugarh and Tinsukia Districts, is densely populated and has recorded a maximum population density of 1178 people per square kilometre, while Sadiya, Dibrugarh West, and Margherita recorded minimum population densities of 122, 125, and 299 people per square kilometre, respectively (table- 4.5).

Table 4.4
Dibrugarh and Tinsukia Districts
Distribution of Population, 1971

Thanas	Total Population	Rural Population	Urban Population
Dibrugarh	2,70,305	2,89,923	80,348
Moran	99,966		
Tinsukia	1,44,947	1,36,092	72,401
Bordubi	63,546		
Chabua	1,70,461	1,36,092	3,888
Doom Dooma	1,98,908	2,52,650	10,510
Sadiya	64,252		
Jaipur	2,03,035	1,84,289	18,746
Margherita	81,937	72,687	9,250
Digboi	1,13,762	81,374	32,388

Source:- Census of India,1971

Dibrugarh And Tinsukia Districts
Thanawise Distribution of Urban & Rural Population
1971

Sl.No   Thana
1   Dibrugarh
2   Moran
3   Tinsukia
4   Bordubi
5   Chabua
6   Doom Dooma
7   Sadiya
8   Jaipur
9   Margherita
10   Digboi

Urban Population
<50,000 Persons
25,000-50,000 Persons
0 - 25,000 Persons

One dot represents 2,000 Rural Population

28°0'0"N
27°30'0"N
95°0'0"E
95°30'0"E
96°0'0"E
Kilometers
0   10   20   40

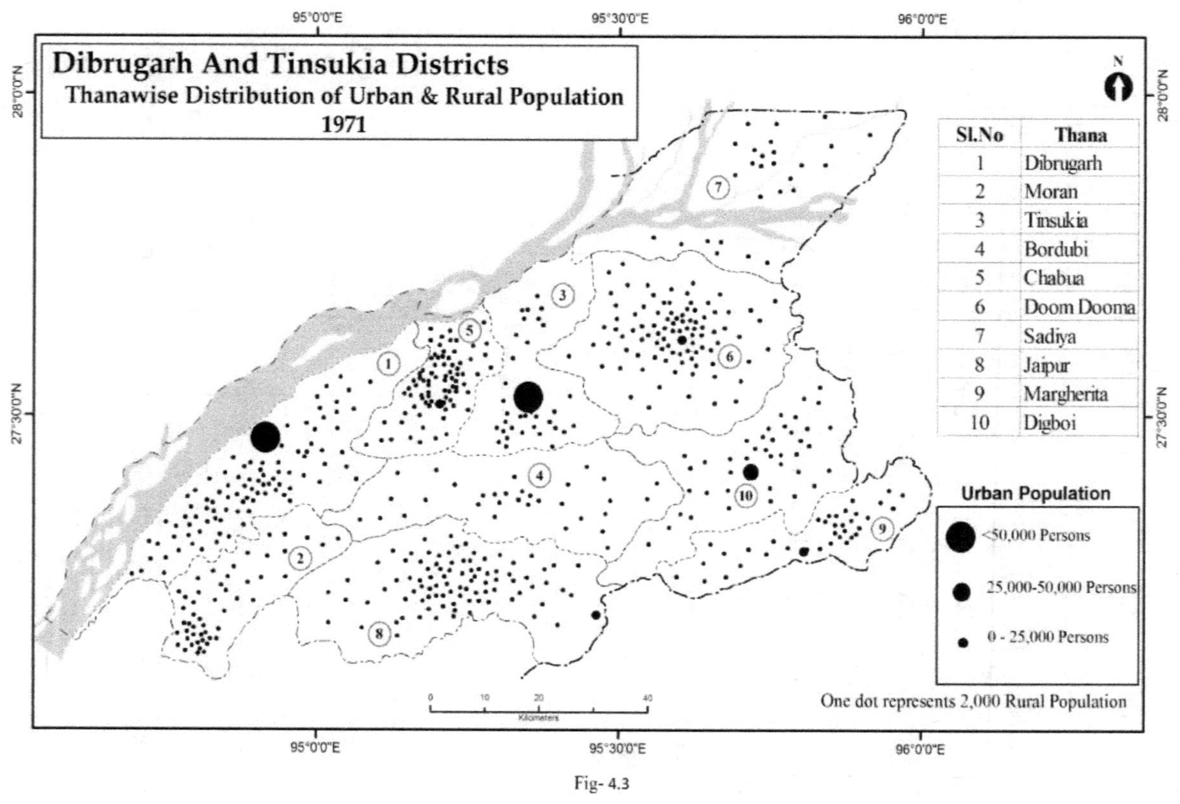

Fig- 4.3

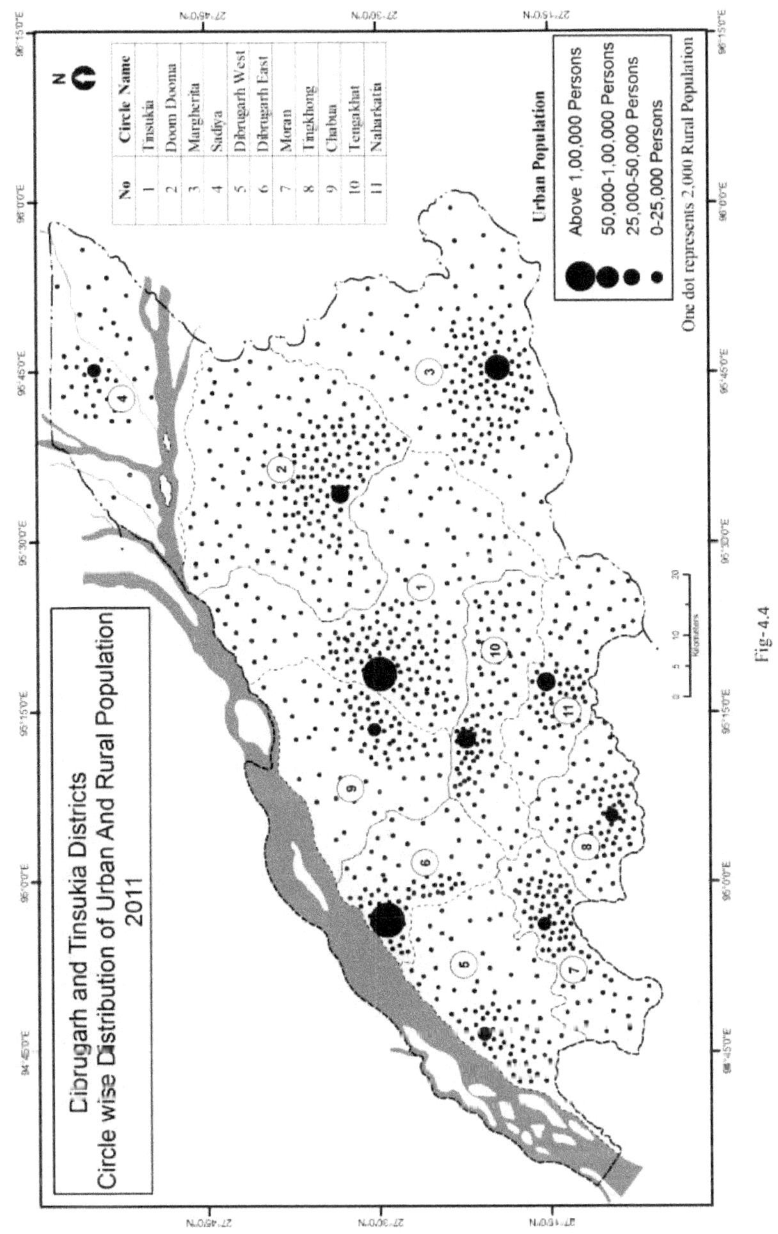

Fig-4.4

Dibrugarh and Tinsukia Districts
Circle wise Density of Urban Population
2011
N
No | Circle Name
1 | Tinsukia
2 | Doom Dooma
3 | Margherita
4 | Sadiya
5 | Dibrugarh West
6 | Dibrugarh East
7 | Moran
8 | Tingkhong
9 | Chabua
10 | Tengakhat
11 | Naharkatia
LEGEND
Persons per sq.km.
0 - 300
300 - 600
600 - 900
900 - 1200
Kilometers

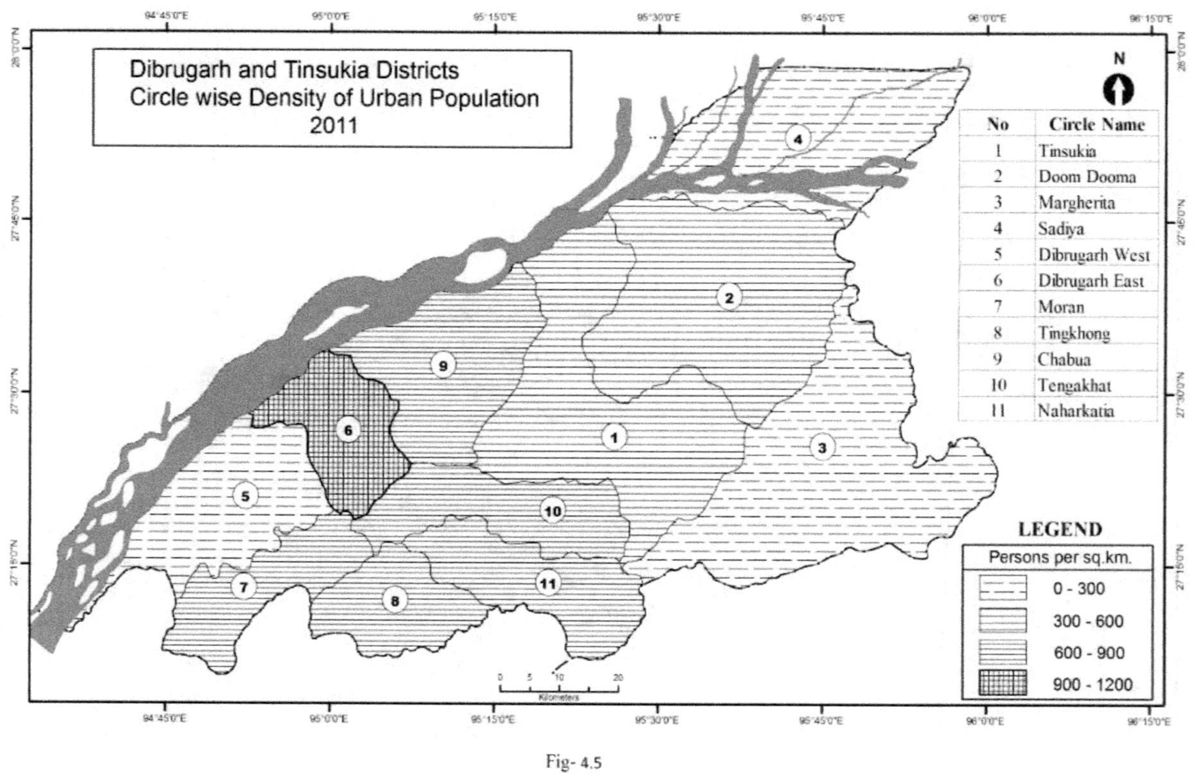

Fig- 4.5

Table-4.5
Dibrugarh and Tinsukia Districts
Circle-wise Distribution and Density of Population, 2011

	Circle	Area	Total population	Urban population	Rural Population	Density of Population
1	Tinsukia	777.44	4,37,341	1,31,664	3,05,677	563
2	Doom Dooma	1002.20	4,14,916	38,344	3,76,572	414
3	Margherita	1233.83	3,69,833	82,682	2,87,151	299
4	Sadiya	776.53	94,858	10,302	84,556	122
5	Dibrugarh West	1279.27	1,59,520	7,136	1,52,384	125
6	Dibrugarh East	228.96	2,69,676	1,46,883	1,22,793	1178
7	Moran	397.51	1,69,801	8,445	1,61,356	427
8	Tingkhong	378.29	1,59,315	0	1,59,315	421
9	Chabua	355.61	1,59,624	8,788	1,50,836	449
10	Tengakhat	346.73	219,749	38,105	1,81,644	634
11	Naharkatia	394.62	1,90,063	34,407	1,55,656	482
	Total		26,44,696	5,06,756	21,37,940	

Source:-Dibrugarh and Tinsukia circle office and census of India, 2011

The population concentration and other demographic characteristics of the districts have been determined using the Lorenz Curve. Regarding inspection, we can get the Lorenz Curve ready for 2011 for both urban and rural populations. The two obtained curves are shown in figure 4.6. The distribution of the urban population is relatively more concentrated than the rural population, according to an analysis of the two curves.

Table-4.6
Dibrugarh and Tinsukia Districts
Lorenze Curve Calculation of Urban Population, 2011

Circle	Total pop	Urban pop	% of urban pop to total pop	% of urban pop. to regional total urban pop	% of total pop. to regional total pop	Cumulative % of urban pop(xi)	Cumulative % of Pop to regional total pop(yi)	Xiyi+1	∑xi+1yi
Tinsukia	437,341	131,664	30.11	25.98	16.54	25.98	16.54	837.34	554.92
Doom Dooma	414,916	38,344	9.24	7.57	15.69	33.55	32.23	1550.35	1607.31
Margherita	369.833	82,682	22.36	16.32	13.98	49.87	46.21	2813.17	3643.66
Dibrugarh East	269,676	146,883	54.47	28.98	10.20	78.85	56.41	5103.17	487.13
Tengakhat	219,749	38,105	17.34	7.52	8.31	86.37	64.72	6210.87	6029.32
Naharkatia	190,063	34,407	18.10	6.79	7.19	93.16	71.91	7297.22	6819.22
Moran	169,801	8,445	4.97	1.67	6.42	94.83	78.33	8000.81	7563.54
Chabua	159,624	8,788	5.51	1.73	6.04	96.56	84.37	8729.02	8265.73
Dibrugarh West	159,520	7,136	4.47	1.41	6.03	97.97	90.40	9446.27	8856.49
Tingkhong	159,315	0	0	0	06.02	97.97	96.42	9797.00	9642.00
Sadiya	94,858	10,302	10.86	2.03	3.59	100	100		
Total	2644696	506756						59785.22	53469.32

$$G = \frac{1}{100*100} \mid \sum xiyi+1-\sum xi+1yi \mid \frac{6315.9}{10000}=0.63$$

The value for the urban population is found to be G=0.63

Table-4.7
Dibrugarh and Tinsukia Districts
Lorenze Curve Calculation of Rural Population, 2011

Circle	Total Pop	Rural Pop	% of Rural Pop to total Pop	% of Rural Pop. to Regional rural Pop	% of total Pop. to Regional total Pop	Cumulative % of Rural Pop (xi)	Cumulative % of Pop to Regional total Pop (Yi)	∑xiyi +1	∑xi+1 yi
Tinsukia	4,37,341	3,05,677	69.89	14.30	16.54	14.30	16.54	460.89	527.79
Doom Dooma	4,14,916	3,765,72	90.76	17.61	15.69	31.91	32.23	1474.56	1461.31
Margherita	3,69,833	2,87,151	77.64	13.43	13.98	45.34	46.21	2557.63	2360.41
Dibrugarh East	2,69,676	1,22,793	45.53	5.74	10.20	51.08	56.41	3305.90	3360.91
Tengakhat	2,19,749	1,81,644	82.66	8.50	8.31	59.58	64.72	4284.40	4327.18
Naharkatia	1,90,063	1,55,656	81.90	7.28	7.19	66.86	71.91	5237.14	5350.82
Moran	1,69,801	1,61,356	95.03	7.55	6.42	74.41	78.33	6277.97	6381.55
Chabua	1,59,621	1,50,836	94.49	7.06	6.04	81.47	84.37	7364.89	7475.18
Dibru	1,59,	1,52,		7.13	6.03	88.6	90.4	8745	8777

garh West	520	384	95.53					.71	.84
Tingkhong	2,19,749	1,81,644	82.66	8.50	8.31	97.1	98.71	9710	9871
Sadiya	94,858	84,556	89.14	3.96	3.59	100	100	0	0
Total	26,44696	21,37,940						49419.09	49893.99

$$G = \frac{1}{100*100} \; | \sum xiyi{+}1 - \sum xi{+}1yi | \; \frac{474.9}{10000} = 0.047$$

The value for the rural population is found to be G=0.047.

Because the curve moves first along the y-axis and then along the x-axis, so that the area between the curve and the line of equal distribution would be very close to the area of the triangle, the above value illustrates a relatively higher concentration of urban population than rural population compared to the total population. As a result, this ratio ranges from zero to one. The formula above can be used to calculate the ratio, often known as Gini's coefficient (G), numerically.

**Dibrugarh and Tinsukia Districts, 2011
Circle Wise Extent of Concentration of Urban and Rural
Population
By Lorenz Curve**

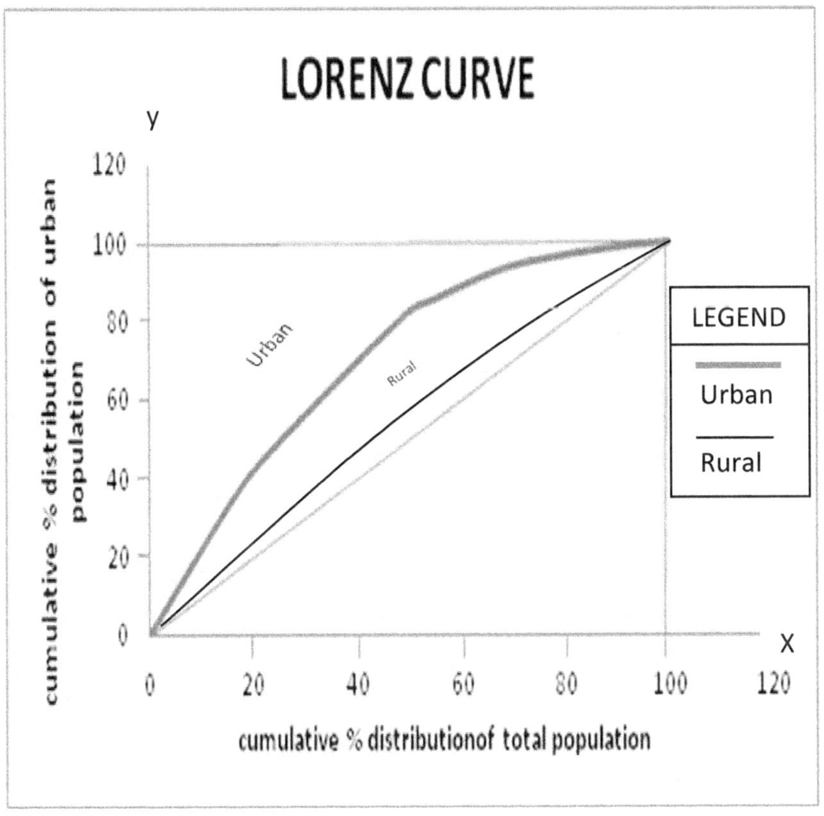

Fig 4.6

The Gini coefficient shows a relatively higher concentration of the urban population than the rural population.

Table-4.8
Dibrugarh and Tinsukia Districts
Urban Centre wise Concentration of Urban Population (L.Q.)
2001, 2011

Urban Centres	1991		2001		2011		L.Q. 1991	L.Q. 2001	L.Q .2011
	Urban Pop.	% of Urban Pop. to total pop.	Urban Pop	% of Urban Pop to total pop	Urban Pop.	% of Urban Pop to total pop.			
Dibrugarh	120,127	35.68	133,571	31.59	145,220	31.38	2.12	1.74	1.79
Chabua	6,104	1.81	17,433	4.12	8,788	1.9	0.11	0.23	0.11
Naharkata	15,052	4.47	15,523	3.67	18,924	4.09	0.27	0.2	0.23
Duliajan	17,017	5.05	23,763	5.6	29,350	6.34	0.3	0.31	0.36
Namrup	19,740	5.86	19,021	4.5	15,483	3.35	0.35	0.25	0.19
Tinsukia	73,918	21.95	101,957	24.12	115,556	24.97	1.31	0.33	1.43
Doom Dooma	15,121	4.49	19,806	4.68	21,469	4.64	0.27	0.26	0.27
Digboi	35,933	10.67	37,143	8.79	33,712	7.28	0.64	0.49	0.42
Makum	11,993	3.56	15,118	3.58	16,875	3.65	0.21	0.2	0.21
Margheria	21,709	6.45	24,049	5.69	26,913	5.82	0.38	0.31	0.33
Moran	-	-	6,826	1.61	8,445	1.82	-	0.09	0.1
Ledo	-	-	8,571	2.03	11,718	2.53	-	0.11	0.14
Chapakhwa					10,320	2.23			0.13
Total pop of urban centres	336714		422,781		462,890				
Total urban Pop of the region	20,04755		23,3513 4		26,44 696				
% of the Urban Population of the Region	16.8		18.11		17.5				

$$\text{L.Q.} = \frac{\%\ \text{of urban population to total population}}{\%\ \text{of the urban population of the region}}$$

In this area, the geographical variance at the district level is particularly extreme. Dibrugarh town's urban population as a percentage of the total population varies from 1.82% in Moran to a high of 31.38% for urban centres. Table -4.8 shows that the district headquarters in the towns of Tinsukia and Dibrugarh has the highest number of urban residents. According to the 2011 census, Duliajan Oil Town, Doomdooma Town, Digboi Town, and Margherita Town all have medium concentration values for the location quotient of the urban population in this area.

Table no-4.8, it is clear that Dibrugarh, Digboi, and Namrup, have a decreasing trend in their concentration of urban population from 1991 onwards. The overall distribution pattern is observed randomly. Among the 13 numbers of urban centres in the districts, only two Dibrugarh and Tinsukia urban centres claim a greater share in the urban scale of the districts including the location quotient above1.00. The remaining entire urban centres have less than 0.5 of the location quotient. It means the general feature of heterogeneous localized concentration of urbanization is apparent in these districts.

Locational Pattern

The fundamental building blocks of urban settlements in a region are "site" and "situation," which combine the physical and cultural contexts. In geographical research, the uneven distribution of objects is a frequent phenomenon that reveals locational properties. Along with the degree of urbanisation, there is an unequal distribution pattern in the urban centres of the Dibrugarh and Tinsukia Districts.

The average urban centre density in the Dibrugarh and Tinsukia Districts was 3631 people per square kilometre in 1971, 5285 people per square kilometre in 1991, and 5806 people per square kilometre in 2001, however, there is a significant range of variance. Urban areas have a population density ranging from 13,910 people per km^2 in Duliajan to 1930 people per km^2 in Digboi Town. The urban center's density exhibits a perfect inverse relationship with the area, meaning that as area increases, density decreases and vice versa when area decreases (fig-4.7).

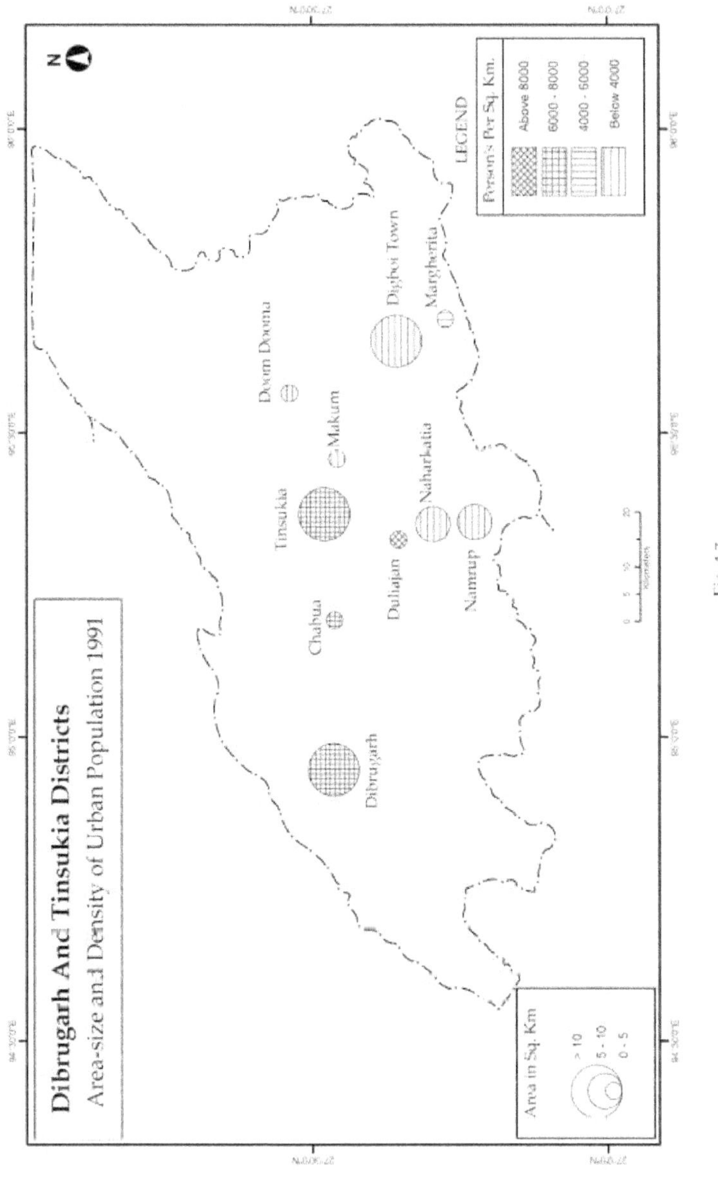

Dibrugarh And Tinsukia Districts
Area-size and Density of Urban Population 1991
N
LEGEND
Person's Per Sq. Km.
Above 8000
6000 - 8000
4000 - 6000
Below 4000
Digboi Town
Margherita
Doom Dooma
Makum
Tinsukia
Naharkatia
Duliajan
Namrup
Chabua
Dibrugarh
Area in Sq. Km
> 10
5 - 10
0 - 5
Kilometers
Fig.-4.7

Table-4.9
Dibrugarh and Tinsukia Districts
Density of Urban Population 1971-2011

Towns	Urban Population				Density			
	1971	1991	2001	2011	1971	1991	2001	2011
Dibrugarh	80343	120127	133571	145220	8034	7750	8617	9369
Chabua	3888	6104	7433	8788	4136	6494	7907	9349
Naharkatia	10774	15052	15523	18924	1488	2079	2907	3544
Duliajan	11497	17017	3763	29350	4599	8065	11262	13910
Namrup	7972	19740	19021	15483	2387	3782	3644	2966
Tinsukia	54911	73918	101957	115556	5300	7013	9673	10964
Doom	10510	15121	19806	21469	4058	3516	4606	4993
Digboi	32388	35933	37143	33712	1854	2057	2126	1930
Makum	5992	11993	15118	16875	1646	3259	4108	4586
Margherita	9250	21709	24049	26913	3003	4619	4117	5726

Source: Census of India 1971,1991,2001, 2011

Spatial Pattern

From the spatial perspective, urban distribution remains a dependent phenomenon to behave in response to the historical, economic, social, and political situation. An examination of the concentration of urban distribution patterns of Dibrugarh and Tinsukia Districts with the help of Location Quotient is shown in table-4.10 in all administrative circles of 2011. The table-4.10 reveals that the concentration of the urban population was higher in the Dibrugarh East circle at 2.84 followed by Tinsukia, and Margherita at 1.57 and 1.17 respectively. Increasing urbanization in the circles of Dibrugarh East and Tinsukia occurs through inter-district and rural-urban migration affecting the rural-urban ratio.

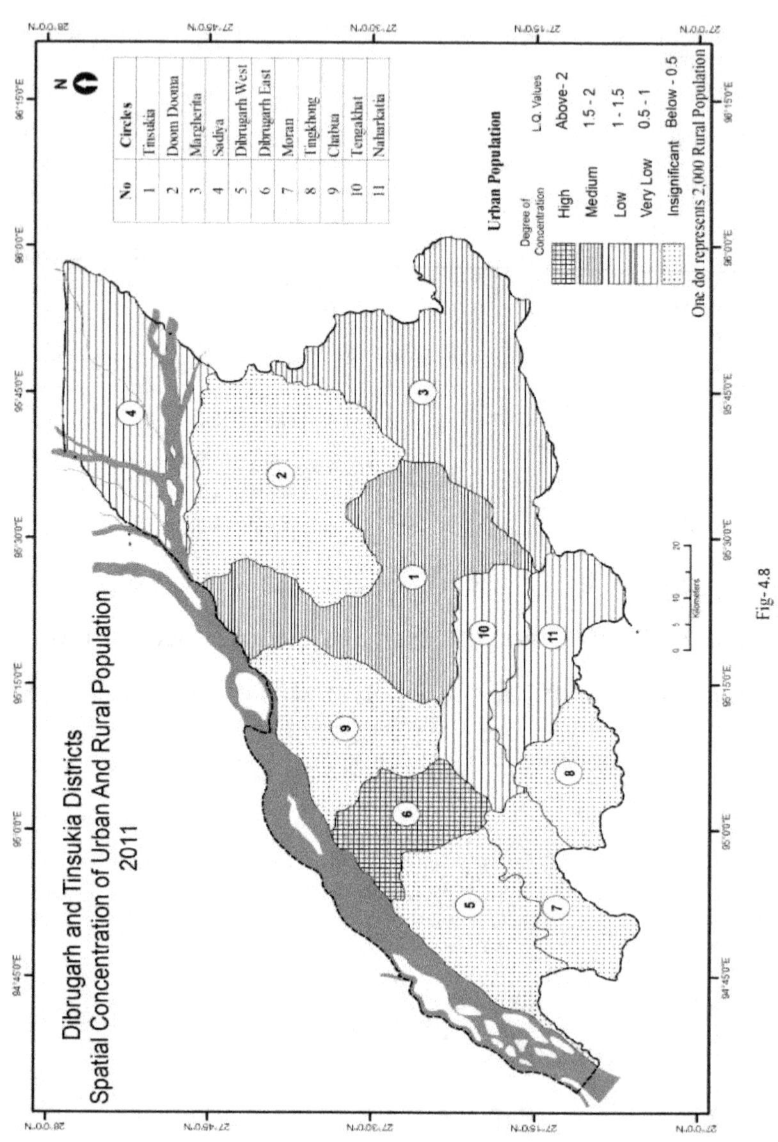

Dibrugarh and Tinsukia Districts
Spatial Concentration of Urban And Rural Population
2011
N
No | Circles
1 | Tinsukia
2 | Doom Dooma
3 | Margherita
4 | Sadiya
5 | Dibrugarh West
6 | Dibrugarh East
7 | Moran
8 | Tingkhong
9 | Chabua
10 | Tengakhat
11 | Naharkatia
Urban Population
Degree of Concentration | L.Q. Values
High | Above- 2
Medium | 1.5 - 2
Low | 1 - 1.5
Very Low | 0.5 - 1
Insignificant | Below - 0.5
One dot represents 2,000 Rural Population
Kilometers
0 5 10 20
Fig- 4.8

Table-4.10
Dibrugarh and Tinsukia Districts
Spatial (Circle wise) Concentration of Urban Population,2011
(L.Q)

	Circles	Total population	Urban population	% of urban population to the total population	% of the urban population of the region	L.Q
1	Tinsukia	437,341	131,664	30.11		1.57
2	Doom Dooma	414,916	38,344	9.24		0.48
3	Margherita	369.833	82,682	22.36		1.17
4	Dibrugarh East	269,676	146,883	54.47	19.16	2.84
5	Tengakhat	219,749	38,105	17.34		0.91
6	Naharkatia	190,063	34,407	18.10		0.94
7	Moran	169,801	8,445	4.97		0.26
8	Chabua	159,624	8,788	5.51		0.29
9	Dibrugarh West	159,520	7,136	4.47		0.23
10	Tingkhong	159,315	0	0		0
11	Sadiya	94,858	10,302	10.86		0.57
	Total	2644696	506756			

Source: Census of India 2011

L.Q.= Location Quotient = (Ax / Ex) / (An / En) where Ax = urban population A in area x, Ex = total population in area x, An = urban population in whole (n) area, En = total population in the whole area.

The districts exhibit, on a spatial scale, a very low to a high level of urbanisation.If they are planned as centres of development, the existing metropolitan centres will sustain the districts' economic possibilities.

5 PROCESSES OF GROWTH AND DEVELOPMENT

History of Urban Growth

Urbanization is a process that manifests itself in changes to demographic, social and economic, and environmental characteristics over time, space, and across sectors. These changes can be seen in the growing concentration of people in urban areas larger than villages, the rise in secondary and tertiary employment, and the gradual adoption of particular social changes that depart from traditional rural societies. The rate of urbanisation is directly related to the degree of social development.

There is no documentation of the growth of urbanisation in the pre-British Dibrugarh and Tinsukia Districts. These areas have long been predominantly rural. The majority of its residents work in the primary sector and typically reside in the villages. Non-agricultural activities, such as trade, commerce, services, transportation, industry, etc., have all developed extremely slowly until recently.

The process of urbanization in the Dibrugarh and Tinsukia districts may be discussed according to the following characteristic time- periods:

1. Pre-British period.

2. British period.

3. Post –Independence period.

There is currently no evidence of any ancient urban centres in the districts. Initially, the Bodos, Chutias, and Ahom consecutively ruled the districts. To defend the regions against attacks by tribes from the mountainous area, the Ahoms constructed a fort (Garh) on the bank of the Dibru, a river that flows into the powerful Brahmaputra. Several capital cities established by the Ahom rulers appeared in the medieval era in areas like Gurgaon, Rangpur, and Sibsagar. These cities were all rural and defined by the palace, which was surrounded by high walls and built up with temples, pavilions, tanks, and other structures. With the events of the development of rail and motor transport, exploitation of forest and mineral resources, expansion of modern education, promotion of tea cultivation, and trade and commercial activities, modern civilization of urban started in the districts. The medieval capital centre like Tinsukia had also changed both spatially and functionally due to trade – cum-railways. British gave much priority to the expansion of transport and communication intending to exploit its rich natural resources. The British promoted foreign investment, particularly in manufacturing. The large-scale movement of tea workers and skilled craftspeople into the regions had also been encouraged by the British authority. Only the tea factories and the Digboi oil refinery are noteworthy as manufacturing facilities in the regions from the British era; modernised agriculture had not been created there. There was hardly any interaction between the rural and urban sectors in the districts. The towns that emerged were essentially centres for commerce, government, and transportation that were governed by outsiders. Dibrugarh, Sadiya, and Tinsukia Cities were developed during the British era. Since 1953, Sadiya Town has deteriorated. It was a lovely town built around a military base (fig 5.1). A military fort and cantonment complex were also present in Dibrugarh Town. The Brahmaputra also undermined the Dibrugarh Town's original centre (fig-5.1). At the Tinsukia railway station, Tinsukia Town was created.

Both the number of urban centres and the percentage of the region's population have significantly increased since independence. At the time of the split, a sizable number of immigrants from outside the nation had arrived and settled in the region's urban, semi-urban, and rural sectors. Moreover, the number of urban centres expanded from 3 in 1941 to 22 in 2011 as a result of development initiatives under five-year plans, decentralisation of government, and economic development. Many urban areas were also lost at this time, including Sadiya Town and a sizable portion of Dibrugarh Town, as a result of the 1950 Great Earthquake or the natural channel shifting caused by the erosion of the Dibang and the Brahmaputra, respectively.

Determinants of Urbanisation:-

1. Economic
2. Social
3. Demographic
4. Transport

i. Economic process:-

The economic elements that contribute to an area's urbanisation are numerous. First off, the districts of Dibrugarh and Tinsukia are extremely wealthy in material resources, including enormous reserves of coal, oil, and natural gas. Towns like Makum, Ledo, and Margherita have been created to produce coal. Naharkatita, Moran, Digboi, and Duliajan towns are created because of the vast reserves of natural gas and petroleum, which are crucial to the region's economic and urban growth.

Suddyah (Sadia) Town
SCALE - 1inch = 1mile.
1931-32 Year.
RESERVE
Source: Administrative office,
Sadiya Frontier Tract

BANK EROSION OF DIBRUGARH TOWN
BRAHMAPUTRA RIVER
River Bank - 1918
River Bank - 1936
River Bank - 1955
River Bank - 1962
River Bank - 1988
MAP NOT TO SCALE
Source: I.N. Baruah & Sons

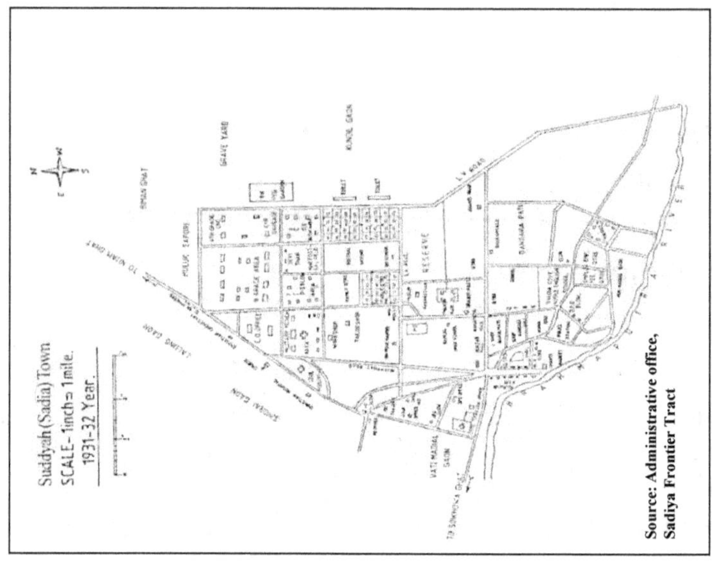

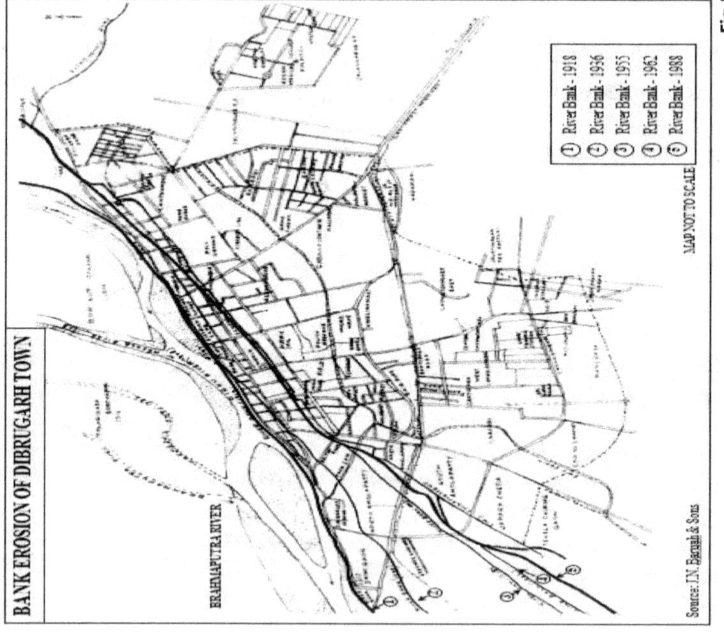

Fig-5.1

Second, trade and commerce volume are primarily related to economic growth. The towns in the Dibrugarh and Tinsukia Districts are primarily involved in the production and exportation of commodities like tea, coal, petroleum, and its byproducts crude oil, natural gas, plywood (previously), timber, etc. These districts have significant deposits of coal, petroleum, and forest wealth. Fertilizers and power are produced and exported by Namrup Town's thermal power plant to the surrounding area. It has been noted that Tinsukia is the sole town where furniture, nails, and tools are made. Among the most significant goods brought into the towns are food grains, medicine, sugar, salt, cloth, pulses, etc.

Thirdly, one of the main methods of urban development is the distribution of commodities and services. Dibrugarh and Tinsukia Districts have 87,153 urban jobs by establishment type, according to the economic census of 2005. The following table displays the inland commerce goods' airport-wise inbound and outbound movements in the districts in 2010.

Table-5.1
Dibrugarh and Tinsukia Districts
Movement of Goods Through Airport, Dibrugarh,2011
(Gross weight in k.g)

To and From Dibrugarh by air	Incoming	Outgoing
Calcutta	290643	24518
Delhi	6729	851
Gauhati	1709	6504
Total	299081	31873

Source: Directorate General of Commercial Intelligence and Statistics, Kolkata

Economic development and urbanisation are closely related, hence urban growth is a necessary part of the development process. The percentage of people living in towns correlates with economic growth as measured by gross national product per person (GNP). The core of the economy is specialisation, which is also thought to be the answer to the causes of urbanisation (Chide, 1950).

Simply said, the primary, secondary, and tertiary production levels relate to the nature of economic activities in a town or city. The type of economic output taking place in the city has a significant impact on the character of urbanisation. The Gross Domestic Product (GDP) for the primary, secondary, and tertiary sectors in the Dibrugarh and Tinsukia districts is displayed in the table below.

Table-5.2
Dibrugarh and Tinsukia Districts
Gross Domestic Product (2003-2004)
(Cost by industry of origin)

Sectors	At Current Price (in lakhs of rupees)
Primary Sector	279074
Secondary Sector	98084
Tertiary Sector	273069
Total GDP	650227
Per Capita GDP (in Rs.)	49360

Source: Directorate of Economics and Statistics, Assam

Whether at the elementary, secondary, or tertiary level, the city and the town are centres of production. Companies produce goods and services as well as jobs. The city's economic activity helps to sustain and expand its population. Larger cities having a wider labour pool, a process of cumulative causation draws in more capital and talent, and towns often continue to grow. As soon as the fundamental threshold for economic functions is reached, economic forces drive acceleration in urbanisation.

ii. Social process:-

India has a long history of urbanisation dating back to 600 BC. The country has had significant socio-cultural impacts over this time that has affected the nature of its metropolitan societies. The Greeks, the Iranians, the Central Asians, Turks, Arabs, and Europeans have all left their cultural marks, among many others.

During the era of transition when the Ahom King lost his prior power and the British rule was cemented, education in Assam was in a rut. Before the establishment of the school in Dibrugarh in 1840, it has been noted that education was essentially unknown in the districts, and it was challenging to locate a man, even among the upper classes, who knew how to write his name.

In Dibrugarh, the first English school was founded in 1840. The next eleven years saw relatively little improvement in the district's educational system. Government schools continued at the same number. Moreover, there was a mission school in Dibrugarh with 78 unsupported students (Govt of India, 1999).

Throughout the following ten years, from 1864 to 1874, the district's entire educational system underwent a significant transformation. Both the number of schools and the number of students roughly ten-fold rose. Only one high school, located in Dibrugarh, served the district. Dibrugarh was home to the only medical school in the province at the time, as well as a survey school where students were trained to be qualified for the position of village. It has been stated earlier that the cause of education suffered a setback in the wake of the upheavals of Moamorias and Burmese inversion which led to the downfall of the Ahom Kingdom. However, the consolidation of the British rules brought about the gradual expansion and improvement of modern education. Several schools were established under state management. Missionaries also took a keen interest in the spread of education and the urge for education was also noticeable among the masses. As a result, several schools of primary and secondary standards came into existence in different parts of the districts. Although collegiate education did not advance much at the time, it underwent a significant increase following the country's independence, particularly during the plan period. These authorities received control of all the local authorities primary schools. Primary education became required in a few particular state regions under the Assam Primary Education Act of 1947. From 1948 until

1959, the district implemented compulsory education in a few designated regions. The area served by this initiative was initially conducted in the Dibrugarh subdivision, which had a total enrollment of 34078 children spread among 420 schools.

Many activities are focused on as a result of the expansion of education and serve as a hub for socio-cultural activities. Eight of the district's towns have hospitals, whereas the other towns only have dispensaries and other forms of health facilities. The town of Dibrugarh enjoys the benefit of housing a prestigious medical school. Urban locations now provide a wealth of opportunities. Urban places are becoming more and more of a focus because success there is easier to come through. Once more, this results in a flood of individuals from all walks of life into the cities.

The table below shows the growth of several institutions and enrolment up to higher secondary classes in 2003-2004 and 2007-2008.

Table-5.3
Dibrugarh and Tinsukia Districts
Number of Educational Institutions and Enrolment
2003-2004 and 2007-2008

	Number of Institutions		Enrolment	
	2003-2004	2007-2008	2003-2004	2007-2008
Primary	2025	2027	204675	137417
Middle	456	801	98597	106951

High School	333	347	29849	48145
Higher Secondary	44	66	7401	7637
Jr.College	5	13	1362	2129

Source: Directorate of Secondary Education, Assam

Religion, language, and geographical background of migrants play a very crucial role in the choice of residence. As a result, the spatial distribution might occasionally represent the socio-cultural and ethnic background, distinctiveness, and segregation. It should be emphasised that the larger communities are typically concentrated in specific locations within the districts. It has been reported that they also like to reside in clusters in some particular places where they may not be the majority, even in the smallest settlements.

Except for Digboi and Chabua Town Committees, all the remaining Civic Bodies in the district registered an excess of receipts over their expenditures during 1978-79, according to administrative data gathered from the relevant Municipal Boards and Town Committees for the financial year 1978-79. The statement demonstrates that in the cases of Dibrugarh, Chabua, Tinsukia, and Digboi Civic Bodies, revenue derived from municipal properties combined with tax collection accounts for more than half of total receipts, whereas in the case of Naharkatiya, government grants combined with money collected from other sources account for the majority of total receipts. Except for the

Dibrugarh Municipal Board, it is noted that no other civic body obtained a loan or advance during this time.

According to the municipal bodies' spending patterns, the general administration alone accounts for more than 50% of total expenditures in the region's four out of eight metropolitan centres with Municipal Boards or Town Committees. When it comes to general administration spending, Naharkatiya tops the list with 89.30 percent of its overall budget, followed by Chabua (66.83 percent), Doom Dooma (63.2 percent), and Digboi (61.2 percent). The lowest share of such expenditure was reported by Tinsukia. The Makum Town Committee's expenditure on public works accounted for the biggest percentage (81.31%), and Tinsukia came in second with 45.18 percent. Spending on public projects reflects where the development process is at.

(iii) Demographic Process:-

Since migration can change a region's demographic and economic balance, it is an important factor. Migration to the districts from adjacent areas as well as from other parts of India can be seen as the most significant contributing factor to population expansion and populating urban centres, above and above rural-to-urban migration.

Many factors, including politics, job, business, education, marriage and family relocation, natural disasters, etc., contribute to migration. Due to its influence on the demographic, political, and socio-economic conditions in both the place of origin and the site of destination, the study of migration trends in any region is given particular attention. According to data from the last century (1901–2001), the establishment and growth of tea plantations, the start of coal and oil mining, the emergence of the plywood industry, and the building of roads and railways all resulted in these districts experiencing the highest growth of the in-migrant population. The districts developed into a financially successful region where new industrial businesses were established in addition to the creation of additional tea gardens, coal and petroleum mining, and railway buildings, all of which attracted a sizable population. Throughout the years 1901 to 2001, the local population grew from 286 thousand to 2,335 thousand

(iv) Transport progress:-

A good transport and communication network is vital for the development and survival of a town. The road, railroad, and other modes of transportation in the Dibrugarh and Tinsukia districts have advanced significantly.

Table-5.4
Dibrugarh and Tinsukia Districts
Length of Roads in Different Categories (in km.)

	Type of Road	Length		Black Topped		Earthen Grave		Total	
		2003-4	2011-12	2003-4	2011-12	2003-4	2011-12	2003-4	2011-12
1	State Highway	218	218	544	1771	1823	1732	2367	3503
2	Major District Road	216	334						
3	Rural Road	1876	2836						
4	Urban Road	57	115						
	Total	2367	3503						

Source: Office of the Chief Engineer, P.W.D Assam

Road transportation is the most important form of human transportation in the Dibrugarh and Tinsukia districts. Individuals can move between the districts while using a variety of services and amenities.

Table-5.5
Dibrugarh and Tinsukia Districts
Habitation Connectivity Status, 2012

District	No. of villages			Total (2+3+4)
	1000+	500+	250+	
Dibrugarh	204	92	68	364
Tinsukia	141	73	57	271

Source: Office of the Chief Engineer, P.W.D (Roads) Assam

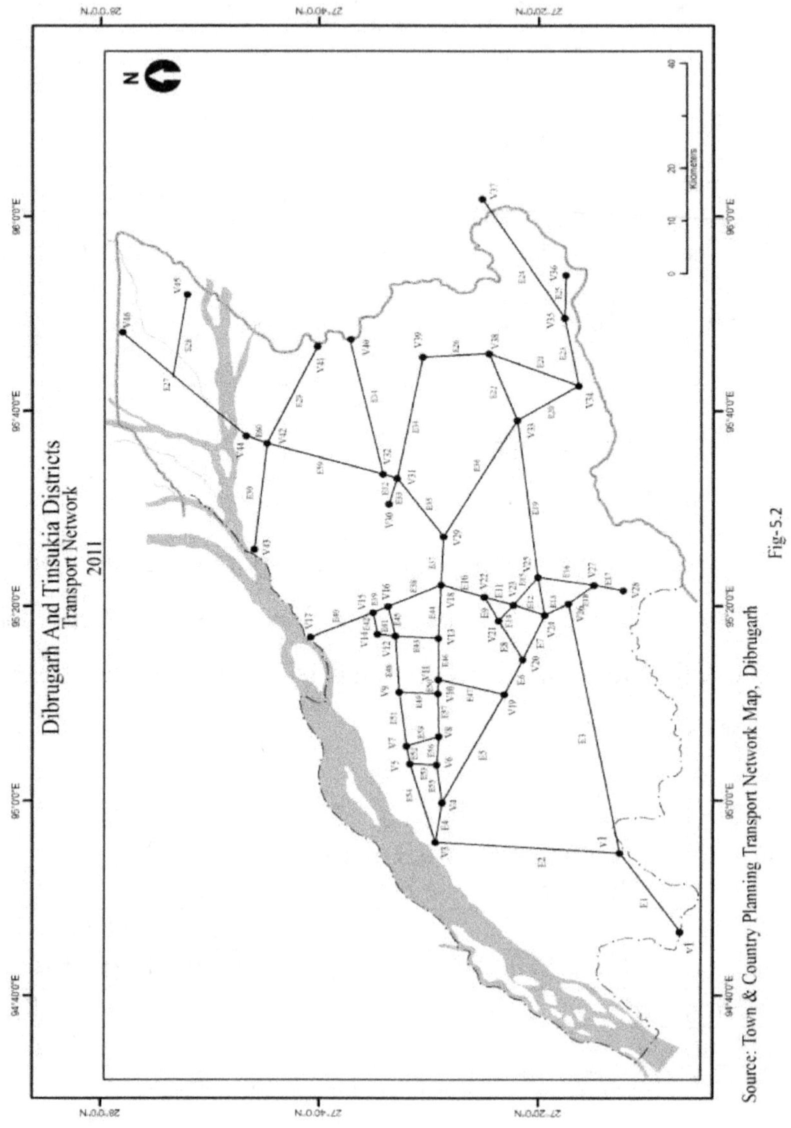

Fig-5.2

Source: Town & Country Planning Transport Network Map, Dibrugarh

The Dibrugarh and Tinsukia districts have an adequate amount of traffic. All roads, except a handful, are congested with traffic. The transportation system in the districts of Tinsukia and Dibrugarh is shown in fig. 5.2. The Dibrugarh and Tinsukia districts have the fewest connecting roadways, according to the research on the transport network (fig-5.2).

Alpha index (α):

$$\alpha = \frac{E - V + 1}{\frac{1}{2}(V^2 - V) - (V-1)}$$

$$\alpha = \frac{60 - 46 + 1}{\frac{1}{2}(46 \times 46 - 46) - (46-1)}$$

$$= \frac{14 + 1}{1035 - 45}$$

$$= \frac{15}{990}$$

$$= 0.015$$

Gama index (y):

$$y = \frac{E}{\frac{1}{2}(V^2 - V)}$$

$$= \frac{60}{\frac{1}{2}(46^2 - 46)}$$

$$= 0.058$$

Where:-

Vertex (v): Where more than one route meets or a road terminates. It could be a crossing or a terminus.

<u>Edge (E):</u> the route joining two vertices is called an edge,

<u>Alpha index (α):</u> In a network with v number of vertices, the maximum number of possible circuits is given by 1/2 (V2-V) - (V-1). The index alpha α is the ratio of an actual number of circuits and the maximum number of possible circuits. The value of α varies from 0 to 1. The value of α=1 shows that the network is completely interconnected as the number of edges decreases the connectivity value also decreases.

<u>Gama index(y):</u> The Gama index (y) is the ratio of the actual number of edges (E) or route connections to the maximum possible number of route connections or edges. In a network with the number of edges as E and the number of vertices as V, the maximum number of possible route connections are 1/2 (V2-V). The value of the Gama index (y) also varies between 0 and 1. When y =0 it means E=0 i.e. there is no edge or connection in the network. The value of y=1 shows the maximum number of connections between vertices in the network (Mahmood, 1986)

There is minimum edge or connection in the network. Road connectivity is minimum but traffic flow is sufficient.

Process of Urban Growth:-

A "place" or specialised area is where non-agricultural land uses are concentrated together with a concentration of people working in non-agricultural occupations in 2004 (Mukherjee and Siddhartha).

Urban centres' growth is influenced by their size, type, and functional scale, including innovations. Several urban patterns could emerge during the dissemination process. Poles may form with arterial/corridor patterns, dispersed patterns, or progressive, occasionally acute distance decline. An urban-rural continuum could result from the dispersion of urban centres.

Subdivisions of the urbanisation process include suburbanization, the growth of the rural-urban fringe, rural urbanism, etc.

Suburbanisation:-

The term "suburbanization" describes the movement of urban characteristics out into the countryside. This is the result of the countryside's haphazard and unplanned development. People living in the built-up region who are searching for less expensive and larger housing are drawn to these areas because the agricultural lands of the outlying villages are transformed for industrial and residential usage. Most urban facilities, like a piped water supply and sewage, are absent from this area. We have also observed this kind of suburbanized area in the districts of Tinsukia and Dibrugarh.

The Dibrugarh university area, Japaragaon and Rajabheta T.E., Tekala Chiring gaon, Chiring gaon, Mahpowalimara gohain gaon to the west, Japaragaon, Khanikar gaon, Dainijan gaon, and Mankata to the south. As a result, they serve as incentives for the development of new, illegitimate housing in Tinsukia Kachujan, Gelapukukhuri Gaon to the north, Loharikachari Gaon, Sukanphukhuri Gaon to the east, Itakhuli Kadamani, Kehang to the south, and New Court Road, Dhekiajuri, and Bahbari to the west. The increased connectedness from the metropolis to other metropolitan centres brought on by advancements in transportation and communication has greatly benefited this current occurrence. Population increase in suburban areas has an impact on the process of urbanisation in the districts (table 5.6).

Table-5.6
Dibrugarh and Tinsukia Districts
Some Suburban Centres of Dibrugarh and Tinsukia Towns

	Suburban	population	Population
	Dibrugarh Town	2001	2011
1.	Mahpowalimara Gohain Goan	986	1,216
2.	Tekela Chiring Gaon	3,737	5,343
	Tinsukia Town		
3	Lahari Kachari Gaon	2,829	3,300
4	Hengaluguri Gaon	1,054	1,336
5	Bajatoli Goan	3,873	4,973
6	Hijuguri Gaon	3,753	5,005

Source: Census of India 2011

Rural urbanism:-

To serve their rural hinterlands, small towns, and major core villages emerge throughout the countryside, a process known as rural urbanisation. These communities more closely resemble rural than urban economies. The majority of the rural communities in the districts of Dibrugarh and Tinsukia are not connected to the urban infrastructure. Because of the poor quality of urban services and amenities, they are sometimes overshadowed by larger centres nearby where they are connected to the transportation network.

Rural-urban Fringe: -

The rapid population growth in unincorporated areas outside the Dibrugarh Town municipal borders (fig. 5.3), in the Dibrugarh and Tinsukia districts, as well as the process of merging into the incorporated sub-suburbs, has been a significant development in urban areas during the past few decades. The urban-rural edge is a continuation of the metropolis. Most land uses are in flux in this area, making them subject to planning and regulation. The "rural-urban fringe" is the area where the area's typically agricultural and typically urban land use structures mix (Richard, 1942).

The periphery never stays still; instead, it constantly expands. A rural area gradually transforms into a rural-urban fringe before eventually fusing with the parent urban centre.

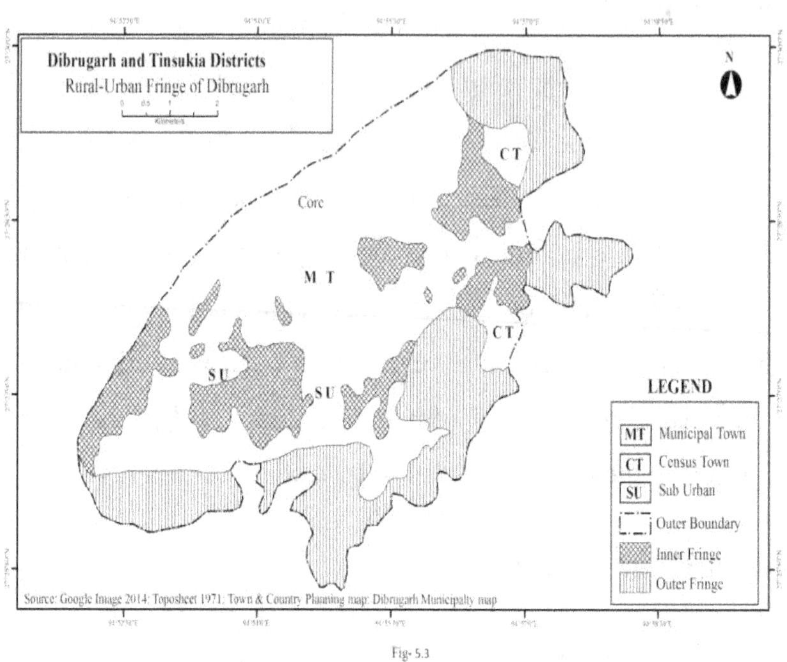

Fig-5.3

Although there is a high population density at the outer edge, there is less strain on the land there due to an increase in non-agricultural occupation. The population density is rising, more people are travelling temporarily, and the area is being developed quickly in the inner fringe. Although there is less population pressure in the periphery, the way that land is used is evolving from subsistence farming to cash crop cultivation and ultimately to non-agricultural use.

The inner edge of Dibrugarh town reaches as far as Mandir Road to the east, Nirmali Gaon to the south, and Dibrugarh

University to the west based on the continuity of the built-up area. The easternmost point of Dibrugarh town's periphery is Barbari (Assam Medical College Area). Up to Japara Gaon and Rajabheta T.E in the west, Boragimoth Kachari Gaon, Nizmancotta in the south, and so forth. The northern boundary of Tinsukia town extends up to Kachujan Gaon, the eastern boundary to Bozaltoli, Lohari Kachari Gaon, the southern boundary to Itakhuli, Kadomoni, and the western boundary to New Court Road, Dhekiajuri. On the other hand, its outside edge reaches as far as Gela Phukhuri Gaon in the north, Sukanphukhuri Gaon in the east, Itakhuli, Khehang in the south, and Nonpuria Koiborta Gaon in the west.

Residents of these locations lead lives that are strikingly different from those of exclusively rural countryside residents and strikingly comparable to those of completely urban citizens.

Present Growth Pattern: A Study on Growth Point:-

By expanding the employment base and introducing a new way of life, the growth points would entice local talent to begin the urbanisation process. These facilities are referred to as growth points or centres for development. Growth spots have their hinterland or sphere of impact. The growing points will have grocery stores, general merchants shops, minor repair facilities, tailor shops, barbershops, restaurants, primary and junior high schools, a sub-post office, co-operatives, community centres, religious temples, railway and bus stations, and other basic facilities. It will also be the headquarters of extension officers such as village-level workers and other minor government functionaries; it will be a focal point for social interconnection where the exchange of ideas will take place and from where development information will spread over to the village. Fig-5.4 shows the 58 numbers of growth points in the Dibrugarh and Tinsukia districts which are playing an important role in rural development as well as converting to urban opportunities in the region. A historic full urban market as well as other facilities can be found at some of the growing points. However, these are not recognised as towns or urban centres in India because they lack the necessary population. These areas of urban growth are numerous and sufficiently large. But these aren't places that belong in cities. So, there is a need for and sufficient room for reconsidering the notion of urban in the Indian Setting.

Table-5.7
Dibrugarh and Tinsukia Districts
Functional Category of Growth Points, 2011

Sl. nos	Growth Points	Functional Category
1	Khowangh at	Agriculture,-Transport, education, tea-related, railway station, trade and commerce, erstwhile river steams ghat.
2	Lepetkota	Industry, transport, radio transmission
3	Barbara	Agriculture, commerce-cum-Transport,

		education, Thana, historical
4	Hatari	Transport, railway, commerce
5	Chowl Khowa	The tea industry, railway station, and education.
6	Bakul	The tea industry, education, research centre (ICMR and others)
7	Lahowal	Industry, Transport, railway station, education, agriculture.
8	Dikom	Oil well, tea industry-related trade and commerce railway station, market (rural)
9	Kazikhowa	The tea industry relates, to agriculture.
10	Panola	Tea factory, trade, commerce, education, railway station, army cantonment.
11	Guijan	Trade and commerce, river steamer station.
12	Borhapjan	The tea industry, Trade, commerce, and railway station.
13	Hansara	The tea industry, Trade, commerce, and railway station.
14	Rupai	Trade and commerce, education agriculture, railway station.
15	Talap	The tea industry, trade, and commerce, thana, railway station.
16	Dangari	Agriculture, education, railway station.
17	Dhola	Trade and commerce, erstwhile railway station, education, transport point.

18	Tingrai much	Trade and commerce, transport, and tea-related
19	Gumtibil	Agriculture, education
20	Natun Balijan	Agriculture, border trade, and communication
21	Santipur	Wholesale, industry, communication, border, and transportation point
22	Dirak gate (Namchaig ate)	Agriculture, education, state border
23	Kakapathar	Agriculture, Trade and commerce, border trade
24	Kumsang	Tea Industry
25	Phillobari	Agriculture, education, tea
26	Tingrai	Tea Industry, oil, gas bottling.
27	Bagapani	Education, railway station, market
28	Golai	Business-cum transportation
29	Bor Golai	Business-cum transportation, coalfield
30	Pengeri	The tea industry, Trade, and commerce
31	Tipong	Coal mining
32	Lekhapani	Tea industry army cantonment, railway station.
33	Tirap	Coal mining

34	Jagun	Business-trade cum-interstate communication
35	Jaipur	Plywood and tea industry
36	Balimarah	Stone Quarry
37	Tipling	Trade, commerce, and oil well
38	Naohalia	Oil wells, agriculture, trade, and commerce.
39	Bordubi	The tea industry, Trade, commerce, education, and railway station.
40	Chariali	Business, trade, and railway station
41	Bhadoi	Business, Nepco thermal project
42	Kathalguri	NEEPCO Power plant and industrial residential area and market.
43	Rajgarh	Business, Education
44	Tengakhat	Agriculture, Trade and commerce, education
45	Tingkhong	The tea industry, agriculture, education
46	Eightmile (Athmile)	Agriculture, hospital, and education.
47	Chunpura	Agriculture, state border point.
48	Dighal Tarang	Tea industry
49	Mohanbari	Tea industry and airport
50	Khalkhati	Tea industry

51	Tiloijan	The tea industry, trade, and commerce, block office.
52	Dinjan	Army cantonment
53	Deomali gate	State border transport, education, forest, tea
54	Main gate	Army and Air force cantonment.
55	Kenduguri	The tea industry, rural market, transport
56	Pithaguti	Transport, education
57	Balijan	Block, education, military cantonment, market
58	Nadowa	The airfield, communication, and shopping.

Source:- Personal field observation

Table-5.7 shows that secondary and tertiary activities account for the majority of the growth points. The primary resources for this region's industrial growth are tea, oil, and coal. Its district headquarters towns predominate all of these expanding centres. These centres are distinguished by population shifts, and the concentration of trade, commerce, and public utility services has grown there as well. The look of modern transportation has changed. All of these point to the fact that the expansion of any urban centre is not the product of a single function, but rather the consequence of the interaction of several forces, each of which stimulates a variety of activities and functions.

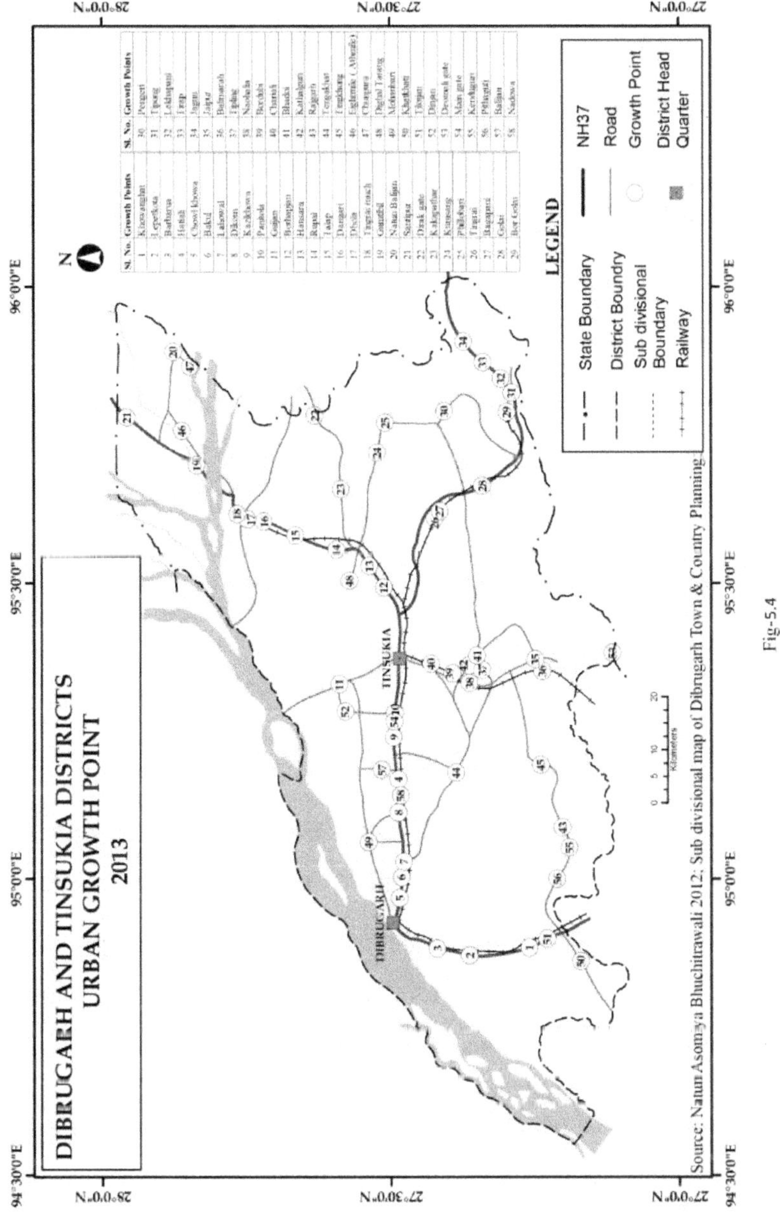

Fig-5.4

Factors of Their Growth:-

According to this study, the following variables account for the majority of growth points in the Dibrugarh and Tinsukia Districts.

(i) Population growth rate: People gradually moving into these places and engaging in activity there, expanding the overall scope of the settlement.

(ii) Percentage of workers engaged in non-agricultural activities: It change in the economy of these areas whereby non-agricultural activities become dominant.

(iii) Size of the growth point:- With socio-cultural facilities acting as magnets to the local inhabitants, the size of this growth point appears to have emerged more for future development.

(iv) Growth of services:- By their very nature, many of these services are centralised in locations that offer administration, catering, and commerce. As more services are required, more people are drawn there, and metropolitan areas progressively expand. Another crucial service that, in the majority of situations, starts at the growth sites is education.

(v) Market forces:- The relevance of sites focused on the market rises as the consumer industry develops. In some of the development areas in the Dibrugarh and Tinsukia Districts, big readymade marketplaces for consumer goods draw new enterprises. These new industries require labour, and labourers in turn expand the size of the potential market.

(vi) Resource factor:- One of the key drivers of growth in this area is resource availability. Resources enable people to increase the value of their products, which in turn enables more people to live and work in the region. As more people move into an area, they need services, which are then given to the populace. The tea industry is expanding and thriving in this area. Large-scale labour is therefore necessary, and as output increases, so does the demand for labour, leading to the agglomeration of people.

(vii) Transport network:- Better transportation infrastructure is shown to boost people's mobility and promote settlement and expansion of activities along important transport routes and halting sites in the growing areas of Dibrugarh and Tinsukia Districts.

Prospects of Urbanization in the Districts:-

To develop the growth points under examination, a perspective strategy is required. The creative urban centres will be the growing areas. They will be connected to sister growth sites by networks of roads or railroads. The study suggests that by supplying and exporting tea leaves, the tea industry may contribute significantly to addressing the growing problem of unemployment. The tasks allocated to the growth points should result in the region's social, economic, and emotional integration.

6 PROCESS OF MIGRATION

The process of population concentration caused by migration:

The districts of Dibrugarh and Tinsukia in India have one of the most diverse populations. It is a region where the vast majority of individuals remain close to where they were born throughout their whole lives. Nonetheless, more people have been relocating from other regions of the subcontinent, notably since independence, which has increased contact between individuals from various cultural, linguistic, religious, and caste backgrounds in Assam's major towns. Nevertheless, it has been noted that many regional linguistic groups have continued to practice their old traditions in metropolitan settings. In the urban centres of the Dibrugarh and Tinsukia Districts, migrants' choices of residence are greatly influenced by their religion, language, and ethnic background. The larger communities are generally concentrated in a few specific districts, and as a result, the spatial distribution might occasionally reflect geographic, and socio-cultural segregation and individuality. It has been observed that even in smaller communities, they prefer to reside in groups in some particular geographic regions where they might not be the majority.

The Trends of Migration

Up to 1921, the number of these immigrants in Dibrugarh and Tinsukia Districts was quite low as compared to other lower Assam districts. Nonetheless, it increased to 19,200 people in 1931. Even after the division of the country, the migration flow continued, and in the former Lakhimpur district, 61,000 people were counted as migrants in 1951 (Govt of India,1999).

In 1961, there were 41,777 Nepalese, up to just 3,717 in 1901. (table-6.1). The majority of Nepalis resided in rural areas. In 1961, there were 1,15,929 Punjabi and Rajasthani speakers in the districts, and 1,902 Marwaries resided in the towns.

In 1961, there were approximately 1,079,000 labourers employed in tea plantations, mines, quarries, etc. The majority of people immigrated from diverse regions of central and northern India, where they primarily made permanent settlements. After 1930, the migration to the tea gardens in the then-Lakhimpur District slowed down, although even at that point, the percentage of immigrants living in the tea gardens reached as high as 25.7 percent in 1951.

Table-6.1
Dibrugarh and Tinsukia Districts
In-migration, 1872-1961

In-migrants		1872		1901		1921		1961	
		Total in migration	P.C. of growth	Total in migration	P.C. of growth	Total in migration	P.C. of growth	Total in migration	P.C. of growth
Foreigners	Europe	125	-	431	244.8	405	6.0	449	10.9
	Asia	14	-	37	164	231	524.3	577	149.7
	Nepal	194	-	3,717	1816.0	6,430	73.0	41,777	545.1
	Bangladesh		-			638		99,417	15,482,6
States of India	Bihar, Orissa, Madhya Pradesh, Uttar Pradesh, Punjab, Rajasthan, etc.	7,729	-	1,23,902	1,503,1	1,84,329	48.8	3,39,033	83.9
	Pre-Partition Bengal &Post Partition W.Bengal	142	-	36,243	25,423.2	42,509	17.3	1,15,929	172.7
Assam	Other Districts	227	-	8,216	3,519.4	7,289	11.3	62,391	756.0
Total – migration		8,431	-	1,72,546	1,946.0	2,41,894	40.2	6,59,573	172.7
P.C. of the total population of the undivide		10.3%	-	60.2%		54.8%		58.6%	

d Lak him pur Dist rict									

(i) Census of India 1921, Vol.III, Assam, Part II Tables,pp.316-319
(ii) Census of India 1961, Assam, Districts Census Handbook,
Lakhimpur, District,p.336
(iii) Hunter, W.W; A-statistical Account of Assam, Vol. I, Delhi PP.306-
308,418-419.
(iv) Allen, B.C: district Gazetter, Lakhimpur, Vol.III.Calcutta, P-71

From 1951 to 1971, an estimated 20 to 25 lakh people from outside the state moved to Assam. According to estimates, Assam received an additional 15 to 20 lakh outsiders after 1971 (Goswami, 1994). According to the 1991 census, 4,56,513 people lived in the districts of Dibrugarh and Tinsukia as migrants, making up 22.77 percent of the total population of the area counted from their place of birth. However, this number increased to 6,20,023 individuals in 2001, making up 26.55 percent of the total population of the area as opposed to 25.50 percent for the entire state of Assam. The migrant population has had decadal growth that is 2.2 times more (35.82%) than the entire population's (16.48%) growth. We can see from table 3.2 that the migration rates are comparatively greater than the migration rates for the state as a whole between 1991 and 2001. The local Assamese population makes up a sizable portion of the migrants in the Dibrugarh and Tinsukia districts region, which contributes to the region's population growth.

Table-6.2
Dibrugarh and Tinsukia Districts
Growth of Population Through Migration, 1991-2001

Year	The population of Dibrugarh and Tinsukia Districts					Migrants from Dibrugarh and Tinsukia Districts					% of Migrants to the total population of Dibrugarh & Tinsukia district	% of Migrants to the total population of Assam
	Persons	Male (in %)	Female (in %)	Net increase	Decadal growth of total population %	Total	Male (in %)	Female (in %)	Growth of Mig ration %	Net Increase		
1991	20,04,755	52.69	47.31	-		4,56,513	44.82	55.18	-	-	22.77	24.13
2001	23,35,134	52.02	47.98	3,30,379	16.48	6,20,023	47.41	52.59	35.82	1,63,510	26.55	25.50

Source: Census of India, Migration Tables vol-1, 1991 & 2001

The pattern of Migration:-

Inter-district migrants have been outnumbered by internal migration in the districts of Dibrugarh and Tinsukia. The percentage share of this type of migration in overall migration, however, increased from 51.97 percent in 1991 to 70.50 percent in 2001, according to a clear pattern that can be seen. However, inter-district migration decreased from 28.46 percent in 1991 to 18.15 percent in 2001 as a result of the decline in employment possibilities in these districts and the growth of other districts, from 28.46 percent to 18.15 percent. From this perspective, a more significant stream of movement is constituted 2volume of migration has interesting implications for urban growth and the level of employment because table no-6.3 shows that rural migration increased from 44.27 percent in 1991 to 54.98 percent in 2001 which leads the prospect of growth of urban population in Dibrugarh and Tinsukia districts.

The majority of interstate migrants entering the Dibrugarh and Tinsukia Districts were from Bihar. West Bengali and Uttar Pradesh migrants came next but in much smaller numbers. Significant numbers of migrants from Tripura and Arunachal Pradesh entered the Dibrugarh and Tinsukia Districts, limiting the movement within the Northeast. Migrations from the other North-Eastern states, on the other hand, were comparatively less significant. As against the popular opinion need for large-scale illegal migration across Assam's international border, the real total number of legal migrants i.e. immigration during 2001 was 7,506 which was decreasing from the 1991 figure 13,160 (table 6.3) to this district. As would be predicted, Nepal was the country with the second-highest number of migrants, after Bangladesh. Larger migrations occur during unrecorded and brief periods, such as a few years, a year, or a few months.

Table -6.3
Dibrugarh and Tinsukia Districts

Percentage of Migrants at various Levels (Migration by Place of last residence)

Migration at different levels	1991				2001			
	Total	% to total	Rural	Urban	Total	% to total	Rural in %	Urban In %
Intra-District	2372260	51.97	44.27	7.70	43713 7	70.50	54.98	15.52
Inter-District	129926	28.46	18.68	9.78	11251 1	18.1	10.05	8.10
Inter-State	76131	16.68	8.34	8.33	62869	10.14	3.73	6.41
International	13160	2.88	1.45	1.43	7506	1.21	0.53	0.68
All Types	456443				620023			

Source: - Census of India, Migration Table, Assam 1991 and 2001 Vol.1 (Table D-1)

Every town experiences two different types of migration: one from rural areas and the other from urban areas. These population migrations are referred to as urban-urban and rural-urban migration streams, respectively. Rural-urban migrants made up 56.88 percent of the region's overall migrations in 1991, while urban-urban (urban to urban) migrants made up 43.12 percent. Following ten years, or in 2001 (table-6.4), there was a 4.29% decline in rural-to-urban migration and a 4.29% increase in urban-to-urban migration. Regarding the decline in rural-urban migration, it has been noted (table-6.4) that the districts have struggled to draw in a sizable proportion of the migrants because of their economy's insufficient size and lack of dynamism, which offers little variety in employment. This may be simply explained by pointing to the expansion of smaller industrial towns like Moran, Namrup, Duliajan, etc. as the cause of the rise in urban-urban migration.

Table - 6.4
Dibrugarh and Tinsukia Districts
Urban Migration in Different Streams-1991 and 2001
(By place of Last Residence)

Streams	% of Migration in Different Streams				Male				Female			
	1991		2001		1991		2001		1991		2001	
	Total	% to total	Total	% to total	Total	% to total	Total	% to total	Total	% to total	Total	% to total
Rural to Urban	667 780	56.88	787 65	52.59	37, 943	59.9	446 01	56.18	288 35	53.33	341 64	48.54
Urban to Urban	506 330	43.12	710 15	47.41	25, 397	40.1	347 94	43.82	252 36	46.67	362 21	51.46
Total	11,7 4,11 0	100	1,49 ,770	100	63, 340	100	79, 395	100	54, 071	100	70, 385	100

Source: - Census of India, Migration Table Vol.1 1991 & 2001. Total = Total migration

The proportion of male migrants was higher than the proportion of female migrants in the rural-urban streams during both periods (table-6.4), but female migrants' proportions increased in the urban-urban streams during both periods due to the social and economic development in urban areas, which encouraged and compelled them to move to towns for jobs, marriage, or for other facilities.

Sex and Migration:-

Migration is largely documented to be sex-selective. In general, there are more male migrants than female migrants, although, in the districts of Dibrugarh and Tinsukia, female migrants outnumber male migrants. 1,63,510 migrants entered the Dibrugarh and Tinsukia Districts, according to the 2001 Census (table-6.5). There are 74,168 women and 89,342 men among these migrants, however, in the censuses taken in 1991 and 2001, the proportion of women migrants to the overall population was consistently greater. Table no 6.5 further shows that the proportion of male migrants climbed from 10.21% in 1991 to 12.59% in 2001, while the proportion of female migrants increased from 12.57% in 1991 to 13.96% in 2001

Table -6.5
Dibrugarh and Tinsukia Districts
Number and Percentage of Migrants

Migrants	1991		2001		1991-2001
	Migrants	% to the total population	Migrants	% to the total population.	Increase in Migration
Total Migrants	4,56,513	22.77	6,20,023	26.55	1,63,510
Male Migrants	2,04,596	10.21	2,93,938	12.59	89,342
Female Migrants	2,51,917	12.57	3,26,085	13.96	74,168

Source: - Census of India, Migration Table Vol. 1, 1991 & 2001

The rise in the percentage of women migrating may be mostly the result of social factors like marriage, and work prospects for men making them the new head of household while rural women remain dependents, etc. Working women today have independent lives at work, in contrast to rural communities. Women have been involved in a variety of economic activities, and particularly in urban areas, there are chances for them to work as cheap labourers in industries including construction, factories, and childcare as well as stores and tea stalls. As a result, the number of female migrants from rural areas has been rising recently.

Causes of Migration:-

According to the census, people migrate within and into the districts of Dibrugarh and Tinsukia for a variety of reasons, including employment, commerce, education, marriage, family movements, and natural disasters. As evident, according to the 2001 census (table-6.6), both Tinsukia and Dibrugarh towns observed that migration among males to seek employment is relatively high at 35.16% from rural and 36.81% from urban to Tinsukia and 35.54% from rural and 33.75% from urban to Dibrugarh town within the districts. However, the increase of females due to marriage appears to be the dominant factor inducing migration with 47.89% and 57.47% respectively from rural and urban migration to Tinsukia town and 55.70% and 51.02% respectively from rural and urban to Dibrugarh town. A major section of the female also migrated to Tinsukia and Dibrugarh towns from rural and from urban in 2001 because of the transfer of residence of the family due to the decrease of the family's old male leader adhered to land. A new generation of male job seekers mentioned in the census has moved with households. According to the analysis above, male migration was primarily motivated by economic factors, but the female movement was motivated by social factors. The causes of this extraordinary exodus from the districts of Dibrugarh and Tinsukia, however, are not examined in the census data.

When additional tea plantations were established, railroads and roads were built, and coal and oil industries were established, many people moved into the Dibrugarh and Tinsukia Districts.

Second, rural areas typically have to relocate to urban areas for this reason due to a shortage of educational facilities, particularly for higher education. Following completion of their studies, a large portion of them relocates to urban areas to make a living.

Lastly, it has been suggested that the best factors influencing migration into the Dibrugarh and Tinsukia Districts are their excellent weather conditions.

Last but not least, migration in these areas was significantly impacted by World War II. The movement of people from the areas outside of Assam has been greatly impacted by the partition of Bengal, the incorporation of East Bengal into Pakistan, the

Liberation struggle of Bengal against Pakistan and the foundation of Bangladesh, natural calamities of Bangladesh, etc. The impact of several popular uprisings and movements in Assam also contributes to the migration's periodic ups and downs.

According to the Statistical Handbook of Assam, there were 763 registered factories altogether in the Dibrugarh and Tinsukia districts in 2006, employing 35,211 people, or roughly 24.4% of all factories and 31.2% of all workers in the state. These areas serve as Arunachal Pradesh's entrance. Not only have transportation and communication advance during the post-independence era, but also trade, commerce, tourism, etc.

Table -6.6
Dibrugarh and Tinsukia Districts
Instant Factors of Migration into Dibrugarh and Tinsukia
Towns as per census,2001

REASONS	SEX	TINSUKIA		DIBRUGARH	
		From Rural	From Urban	From Rural	From Urban
Employment	Male	35.16 (4390)	36.81 (1668)	35.54 (3506)	33.75 (1535)
	Female	2.70 (208)	3.08 (146)	3.95 (390)	3.98 (205)
Business	Male	29.71 (3710)	21.39 (969)	20.71 (2043)	14.49(659)
	Female	1.17 (90)	0.82 (39)	11.40 (87)	0.72 (37)
Education	Male	0.75 (94)	1.04 (47)	5.23 (516)	2.95 (134)
	Female	0.48 (37)	0.44 (21)	4.06 (310)	2.12 (109)
Marriage	Male	0.43 (54)	4.41(20)	0.61 (60)	0.99 (45)
	Female	47.89(3696)	57.47 (2723)	55.70(4251)	51.02(2629)
Moved after Birth	Male	1.46 (182)	3.20 (145)	1.95 (192)	1.36 (62)

	Female	1.35 (104)	1.79 (85)	1.23 (94)	0.70 (36)
Moved with household	Male	14.38 (1796)	18.73(849)	11.64 (1148)	17.06 (776)
	Female	28.34 (2187)	20.85 (988)	16.69 (1274)	18.63(960)
Other	Male	18.10 (2260)	18.38 (833)	24.33 (2400)	29.40(1337)
	Female	18.08 (1395)	15.53 (736)	16.06 (1226)	22.84(1177)
All Categories	Male	12486	4531	9865	4548
	Female	7717	4738	7632	5153

Source: - *Census of India, Migration Table Vol. 1, 2001*

Migrants are drawn to the districts because of this economic advantage and the expansion of the industrial sector. The Dibrugarh and Tinsukia districts see a significant influx of migrants from other districts in the state as well as from other regions of the country as a result of all these combined circumstances.

Migration From outside:

The movement of migrants is significantly influenced by distance. As the distance grows, fewer people migrate to a place. The proportions of rural-urban and urban-urban migration within the districts are higher than the migration from other districts and outside of Assam in both the 1991 and 2001 years, according to an analysis of migration streams and distance to the Dibrugarh and Tinsukia Districts.

Table -6.7
Dibrugarh and Tinsukia Districts
Distance and Streams of Migration

The extent of Districts of migration	Rural-Urban Migration				Urban-Urban Migration			
	1991		2001		1991		2001	
	Total	P.C.	Total	P.C.	Total	P.C.	Total	P.C.
Within Dibrugarh and Tinsukia Districts	17554	26.29	29839	37.88	17536	34.63	385710	54.31
Other districts of Assam	24291	36.38	23727	30.12	20156	39.81	21227	29.89
Other States of India	24933	37.24	251990	31.99	129410	25.56	11220	15.80

Source: - Census of India, Migration Tables 1991 and 2001

According to the survey, between 1991 and 2001, the percentage of people who moved to Dibrugarh and Tinsukia Districts from other districts decreased from 36.38 percent to 30.12 percent and from 39.81 percent to 29.89 percent, respectively (table no-6.7). Moreover, migrants moving from rural to urban and urban to urban areas are declining (table no-6.7). The increase in rural-urban migration from different places within Dibrugarh and Tinsukia Districts from 26.29 percent in 1991 to 37.88 percent in 2001 is remarkable. An increase is noticeable in respect of urban-urban migration from a different town within Dibrugarh and Tinsukia Districts from 34.63 percent in 1991 to 54.31 percent in 2001 is also due to the results of pull factors. The poor people of near town fringe generally come to settle in the slum areas and work as thela pullers, a rickshaw pullers, vegetable sellers, daily paid labourers, etc. In this way, for better economic opportunities, educational purposes, and service purposes some service holders permanently shifted their residence with their families to other towns within the districts. The decrease in the proportion of migration from different districts of Assam is due to the slow increase of similar facilities in their home districts as time passes. According to the 1991 and 2001 censuses Dibrugarh and Tinsukia Districts received the maximum number of migrants from Bihar (46.95 % & 45.53%) followed by Uttar Pradesh (18.65 % & 16.67), West Bengal (8.59% & 8.37%), Rajasthan (5.83% & 3.60%), Tripura (4.82% & 3.82%), Andhra Pradesh (2.33 & 3.03). Arunachal Pradesh (0.98 and 3.51) in respective years (fig-6.1 & Appendix-6.1). These immigrants work as Rickshow and Thela pullers, coolies, washers, barbers, and cobblers, as well as in the building and road construction sectors and stores, among other jobs. They stayed in the town for a lengthier period after arriving in the area.

DIBRUGARH AND TINSUKIA DISTRICTS: MIGRANTS FROM OTHER STATES, 1991 AND 2001
45000
40000
35000
30000
25000
20000
15000
10000
5000
0
TOTAL MIGRANTS
1 5 8 11 15 18 21 24 27 30 33
States & Union Territories
1991 Total Migrants
1991 In % to Total migrants population
1991 Total Rural Migrants
1991 Total Urban migrants
2001 Total Migrants
2001 In % to Total migrants population
2001 Total Rural Migrants
NO. OF STATES & U.T
(As per Appendix-4.1)

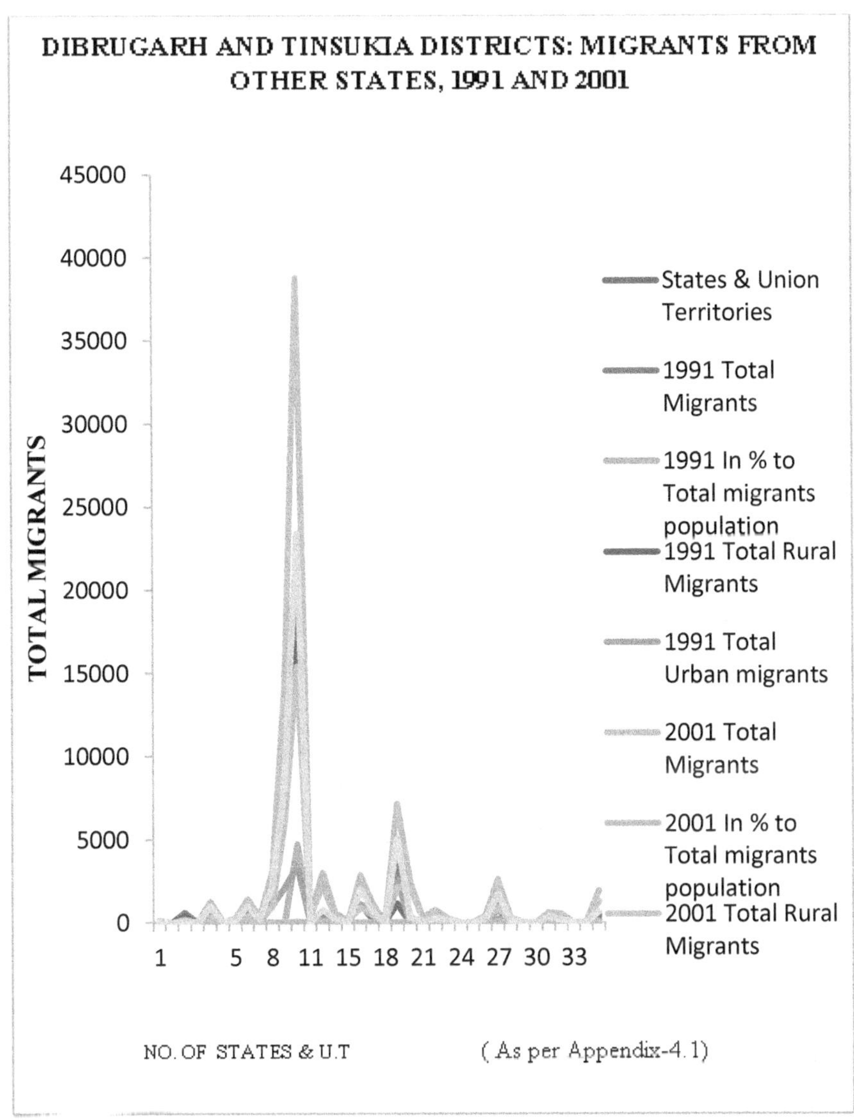

Fig-6.1

7 DEMOGRAPHY, SOCIAL AND OCCUPATIONAL STATUS OF URBAN CENTRES

Urban Demographic Change and Structure:

Dibrugarh and Tinsukia Districts' population structures share several social and economic traits. It comprises age, sex, literacy, education, and other demographic traits that are significantly influenced by a settlement's economic behaviour.

Age-Structure:-

Age structure is a biological population trait. A population's age distribution is primarily affected by three factors: fertility, mortality, and migration. The age-sex composition of a population is one of its most significant demographic traits. It reveals the region's socio-economic and demographic health. In Dibrugarh and Tinsukia Districts, the birth rate is still quite high, similar to that of India and other emerging nations. Due to this, there are a disproportionately large number of kids in the districts. The distribution of a population's members among different age groups is referred to as its age structure. Age-sex pyramids visually represent these data to aid in comprehension and case comparison. The age structure is shown graphically as an age pyramid, where the comparatively wide base represents the number of children and the peak is the nature of the increase of life and death as per age. A population is considered "young" if its age structure has a very broad base and a sharp, narrow peak, and "ancient" if its base is just slightly wider than the remainder of the pyramid.

Table-7.1
Dibrugarh and Tinsukia Districts
Dibrugarh Urban Area
Age – Sex Structure 2011

Age Group	Population	P.C.	Male	P.C.	Female	P.C.
0-4	15894	6.52	8235	6.53	7659	6.51
5-9	18000	7.39	9275	7.35	8725	7.42
10-14	19856	8.15	10327	8.19	9529	8.10
15-19	21530	8.83	11037	8.75	10493	8.92
20-24	23729	9.74	11685	9.26	12044	10.24
25-29	24089	9.88	11788	9.35	12301	10.46
30-34	21383	8.77	10754	8.53	10629	9.04
35-39	21534	8.84	10823	8.58	10711	9.11
40-44	18606	7.63	9746	7.73	8860	7.53
45-49	17150	7.04	9201	7.29	7949	6.76
50-54	13292	5.45	7686	6.09	5606	4.77
55-59	9390	3.85	5479	4.34	3911	3.33
60-64	7320	3.00	3876	3.07	3444	2.93
65-69	4645	1.91	2426	1.92	2219	1.89
70-74	3268	1.34	1755	1.39	1513	1.29
75-79	1859	0.76	974	0.77	885	0.75
80+	2055	0.84	987	0.78	1068	0.91
Age not state	130	0.09	81	0.06	49	0.04
All Ages	243730		126135		117595	

Source: Census of India 2011, Age Group Data, Dibrugarh District, ASSAM

Dibrugarh and Tinsukia Districts
Dibrugarh Urban Area
Age – Sex Pyramid, 2011

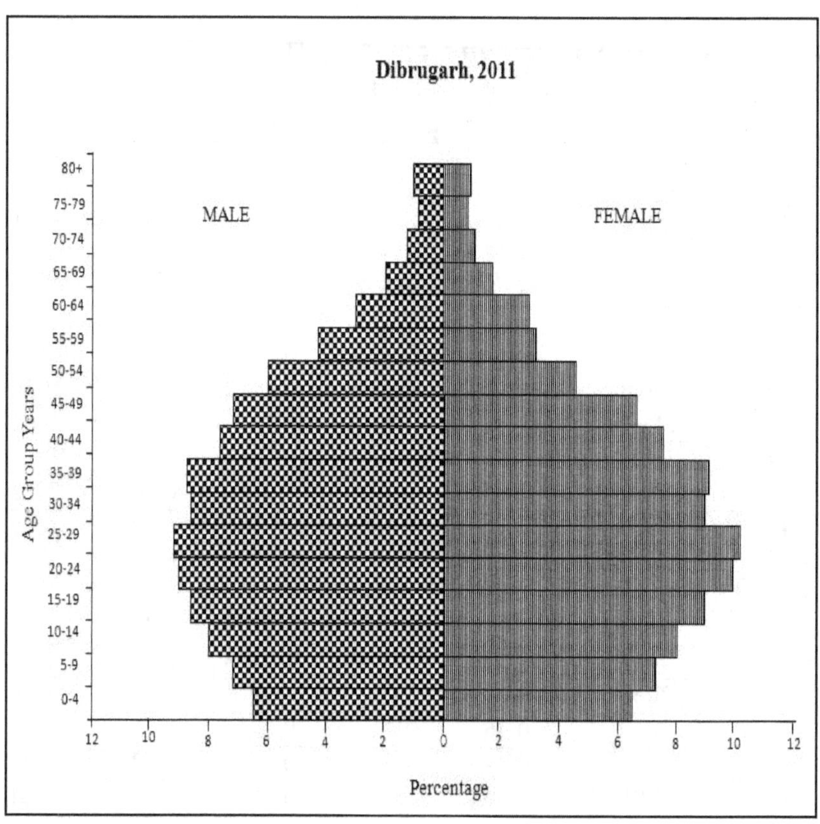

Fig-7.1

Many factors are revealed by the age-sex structure and pyramid from 2011, which shows the age and sex composition of the urban population in the urban areas of Tinsukia and Dibrugarh.

144

Tables 7.1 and 7.2 reveal that in the region with the lowest newborn fertility, children under the age of four made up 6.7 percent of the total urban population. In comparison to state levels, child mortality was quite low, and more than 22% of the population survived before the age of 15 (young). The majority of the time, it occurs in developing nations when population growth is either zero or negative.

Table-7.2
Dibrugarh and Tinsukia Districts
Tinsukia Urban Area
Age – Sex Structure 2011

Age Group	Population	P.C.	Male	P.C.	Female	P.C.
0-4	18314	6.92	9547	6.88	8767	6.96
5-9	21140	7.99	10987	7.91	10153	8.06
10-14	23310	8.80	12212	8.80	11098	8.81
15-19	24029	9.08	12477	8.99	11552	9.18
20-24	25740	9.72	12855	9.26	12885	10.23
25-29	25371	9.58	12685	9.14	12686	10.08
30-34	22665	8.56	11582	8.34	11083	8.80
35-39	22836	8.63	11951	8.61	10885	8.65
40-44	19656	7.42	10517	7.58	9139	7.26
45-49	17843	6.74	9738	7.01	8105	6.44
50-54	13671	5.16	7983	5.75	5688	4.52
55-59	9430	3.56	5470	3.94	3960	3.15
60-64	7818	2.95	4246	3.06	3572	2.84
65-69	4885	1.85	2539	1.83	2346	1.86
70-74	3594	1.36	1827	1.32	1767	1.40
75-79	2068	0.78	1084	0.78	984	0.78
80+	2271	0.86	1083	0.78	1188	0.94
Age not state	102	0.04	53	0.04	49	0.04
All Ages	264743		138836		125907	

Source: Census of India 2011, Age Group Data, Dibrugarh District, ASSAM

Men and women working in areas including transportation and manufacturing, as well as those attending technical schools, colleges, and other educational institutions, make up the little growth in the population between the ages of 20 and 40 (adults). Because of improving working conditions and the availability of medical services, the population of people over 40 is gradually declining, which indicates decreasing mortality among the adult population.

Dibrugarh and Tinsukia Districts
Tinsukia Urban Area
Age – Sex Pyramid, 2011

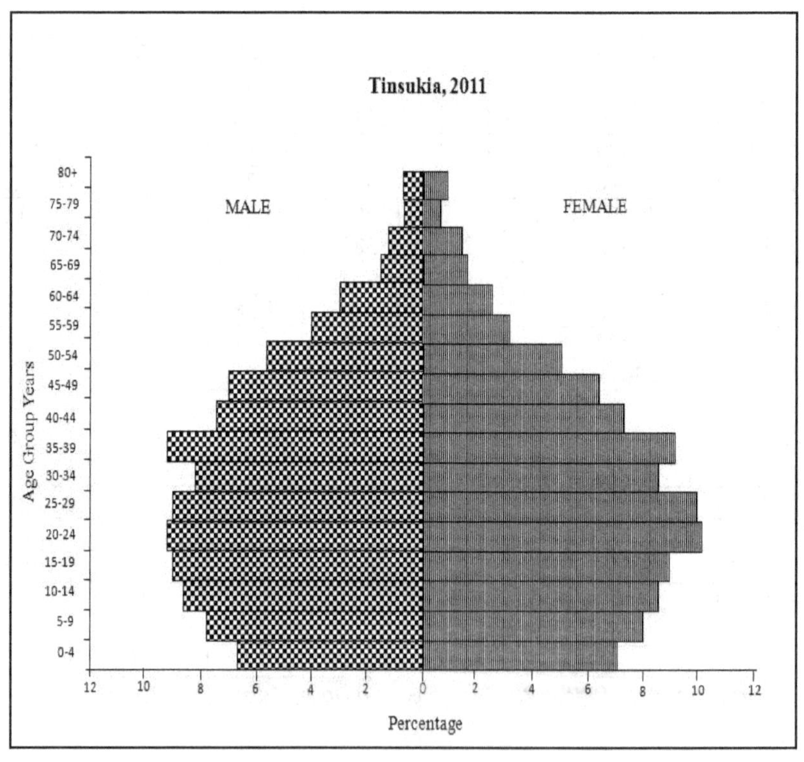

Fig-7.2

Once more, the region has a lower number of seniors and those over 60, which suggests that the mortality rate is higher there. These statistics clearly show that the population's age distribution is unbalanced.

Sex Ratio:

Indicators of population composition that reflect social class in urbanisation include the sex ratio. The sex ratio also reveals patterns and trends in the distribution of females and boys. In the area from 1991 to 2011, the ratio of females to males varied between 742 and 995 per thousand. Despite being the top two towns in this region in terms of ranking, Dibrugarh and Tinsukia have the lowest sex ratios of all the towns. In these urban centres, where a higher percentage of male temporary migrants than females arrive from time to time, migration is one of the main causes of the low sex ratio. Men participate more actively in migration than women do, which causes this. Throughout the years 2001 to 2011, Tinsukia (858) and Duliajan (879) both had low female sex ratios (Table-7.3). In recent years, a recovery trend has become apparent.

Table -7.3
Dibrugarh and Tinsukia Districts
Sex ratio: Females per Thousand Males

Towns	1991	2001	2011
Tinsukia	743	812	858
Doom Dooma	742	820	934
Makum	852	894	934
Margherita	852	894	952

Digboi	846	888	986
Chabua	779	594	969
Dibrugarh	824	878	925
Duliajan	849	918	879
Naharkatia	807	879	934
Namrup	840	867	911
Moran	860	876	918

Source: Census of India,1991, 2001 and 2011 Primary Census Abstrac
Population Tables

Dibrugarh and Tinsukia Districts
Sex Ratio: Females per Thousand Males.
1991, 2001 and 2011

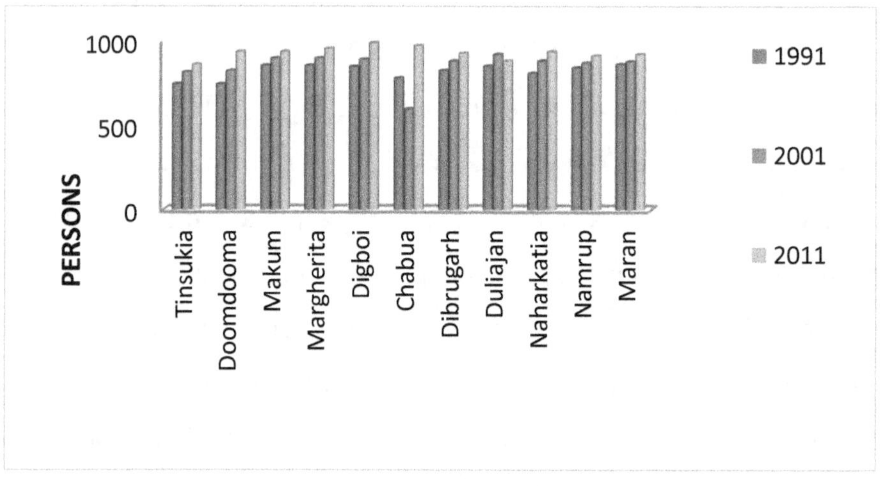

Fig-7.3

Social Status of Urban Population Through Time and Space:

The urbanised region of Dibrugarh and Tinsukia Districts in Assam is 119 years old. The analysis of the social makeup and traits of the many ethnic groups in this area will highlight certain crucial traits.

Religious Composition:

The district's religious makeup had no discernible impact between 1881 and 1891. Out of a total population of 1,79,824 people, 92.2 percent were Hindus, 3.4 percent were Muslims, 3.4 percent were Animists (mainly tea garden labourers), and 2.9 percent were members of other religions. Out of the total urban population of 2,27,530 (16.1%) in the Dibrugarh and Tinsukia Districts in 1971, the Sikhs make up the biggest proportion of 70.9%, followed by the Jains (64.8%), Muslims (46.0%), Hindus (15.5%), Buddhists (9.0%), and Christians (4.2%). (table-7.4).

Table-7.4
Dibrugarh and Tinsukia Districts
Rural-Urban Distribution of the Religious Groups,1971

	Religion	Total		Rural		Urban	
		Population	P.C	Population	P.C	Population	P.C
1	Hindu	13,03932	92.4	11,02,279	84.5	2,01657	15.5
2	Christian	49,566	3.5	47,483	95.8	2,083	4.2
3	Muslim	43,670	3.1	23,574	54.0	20,096	46.0
4	Buddhist	9,882	0.7	8,990	91.0	891	9.0
5	Sikh	2,807	0.2	818	29.1	1,989	70.9
6	Jain	1,263	0.1	445	35.2	818	64.8
	Total	14,11,119	100.00	11,83,589	83.9	2,27,530	16.1

Source: Directorate of Census Operation, Assam, Unpublished Data, 1971

The data at the town level about the religious composition are not accessible. Hindus are the largest religious group in Dibrugarh and Tinsukia Districts as a whole, followed by Muslims in Dibrugarh District but Christians in Tinsukia District. The third religious group is comprised of Christians in Dibrugarh District and Muslims in the Tinsukia District sub-regions. In contrast to other religious groups, it is evident that the Hindu population share will decline in the districts starting in 1991. Hindus are not declining, although their fraction of the population as a whole is other religious groups have increased, but not much.

Table- 7.5
Dibrugarh and Tinsukia Districts
Percentage of Religious Population(1991 and 2001)

	Dibrugarh District		Tinsukia District	
Religion	1991	2001	1991	2001
Hindus	91.30	90.79	90.18	89.48
Muslim	4.49	4.50	3.13	3.48
Christians	1.52	3.80	2.32	5.43
Sikhs	0.15	0.22	0.14	0.20
Buddhists	0.24	0.35	0.33	1.19
Jains	0.06	0.07	0.05	0.08
Other Religious & persuasions	0.10	0.21	0.10	0.10
Religion Not Stated	0.07	0.06	0.06	0.04

Source: Census of India, 1991 and 2001, Primary Census Abstract, Population Tables

Muslims in upper Assam are concentrated in urban areas and their surroundings. In tea garden areas, there is an increase in Christians. There are Hindus in both rural and urban areas, Sikhs and Jains only in cities, and tribal Buddhists only in rural areas.

Language Composition:-

Out of India's four major linguistic divisions, including Austro-Asiatic, Tibeto-Chinese, Dravidian, and Indo-Aryan, the region exhibits a predominance of speakers of Austro-Asiatic, Tibeto-Chinese, and Indo-Aryan. According to the region's linguistic makeup in 1872, Assamese was spoken by around 62.1% of the people as a whole. According to table-7.6, the percentage of Assamese speakers increased nominally by 1.7 percent during a century, from 62.1 percent in 1872 to 63.8 percent in 1971. Yet, the population of Hindi and Bengali speakers increased dramatically, by 2,040.5 and 1,098.1 times, respectively, compared to the region's overall population growth of only 17.2 times. People who spoke Austro-Asiatic languages increased in number by 45 times, while those who spoke Nepali, Rajasthani, Urdu, Punjabi, English, and other languages together increased in number by 34 times, Assamese increased in number by 10.0 times, and speakers of indigenous tribal languages increased in number by only 3.9 times over the century (1872-1971). It implies that there was a different flow of immigration throughout this time.

Assamese speakers make up 82.41 percent of the population in   Dibrugarh District and 58.36 percent in Tinsukia District, followed by Hindi speakers and Bengali speakers, respectively (table 7.7). Smaller populations speak Nepali, Oriya, Punjabi, Telugu, Urdu, and Gujarati. There are also a few extremely small language-speaking communities, but their numbers are relatively few. Although there are no data at the town level available regarding the distribution of languages in this region, it is evident from the observation that the towns of this region are an amalgamation of many communities from many Indian states. Assamese, Hindi, and Bengali are the most widely spoken languages in the towns of Dibrugarh and Tinsukia Districts. Residents of the town's vicinity are primarily Assamese, Bengali, Rajasthani, Bihari, and many Marwari. A few Punjabi families have also long since resided in the towns.

Table-7.6
Dibrugarh and Tinsukia Districts
Linguistic Composition, 1872-1971

Langu ages	1872		1881		1901		1951		1961		1971	
	Pop ulati on	%.	Popu latio n	%	Popu latio n	%.	Popu latio n	%.	Popu latio n	%.	Pop ulati on	%.
Assam ese	50,9 67	6 2 1	69.5 11	5 5. 1	95,9 85	5 5. 5	3,71, 299	4 6. 5	6,60, 107	5 8. 6	8,00 ,160	6 3 8
Indige nous Tribal	19,8 83	2 4. 2	24,1 27	1 9. 1	31,6 98	1 1. 1	54,1 77	6. 8	62,1 53	5. 5	76,7 77	5. 4

Languages												
Bengali	142	0.2	13,421	10.6	36,243	12.6	60,220	7.5	1,15,929	10.3	1,55,926	11.0
Hindi	78	0.09	-	-	-	-	44,000	5.5	99,414	8.8	1,59,157	11.3
Austro-Asiatic Languages	7,535	9.2	11,839	9.4	1,15,477	40.3	22,33,30	29.2	1,33,378	11.8	-	-
Nepali	194	0.2	535	0.4					40,547	3.6	76,777	5.4
Rajasthani	57	0.07	399	0.3					2,984	0.3	-	
Urdu			1,960	1.6					5,044	0.4	-	
Maria	596	0.7							6,899	0.6	-	
Others	2,657	3.2	4,351	3.4	7,211	2.5	35,742	4.5			42,313	3.0

Sources (i) Census of Assam 1881, Report, Table IX
(ii) Census of India 1951. Assam, Lakhimpur, Districts Census handbook, PP.279-283c
(iii) Census of India 1961 Vol III, Assam, Part I-A, General Report p.210
(iv) Census of India 1961 Vol III, Assam, District Census Handbook, Lakhimpur, pp. 336-343
(v)hunter, W.W. 1879 rep. 1975, A Statistical Account of Assam, Vol.I., Delhi, P305,417.
(vi) allen, B.C. 1905: District Gazetter, Lakhimpur, Vol.III. Calcutta, P.12.
(vii) Census of India 1971, Statistics of Assam, Part I-A, General Report,p,90-91

Table -7.7
Dibrugarh and Tinsukia Districts
Language Composition, 1991

LANGUAGE	Dibrugarh District	Tinsukia District
Assamese	82.41	58.36
Bengali	5.62	10.83
Gujarati	0.08	0.31
Hindi	7.42	13.43
Kanaada	0.0029	0.00041
Kashmiri	0.00058	0.0010
Konkani	0.0047	0.0025
Malayalam	0.09	0.021
Manipuri	0.074	0.070
Marathi	0.0089	0.0029
Nepali	1.537	7.91
Oriya	0.62	3.90
Punjabi	0.21	0.22
Sanskrit	-	0.0001
Sindhi	0.0035	0.0064
Tamil	0.0149	0.017
Telugu	0.188	0.94
Urdu	0.022	0.13

Source: Census of India, 1991 Primary Census Abstract, Population Tables.

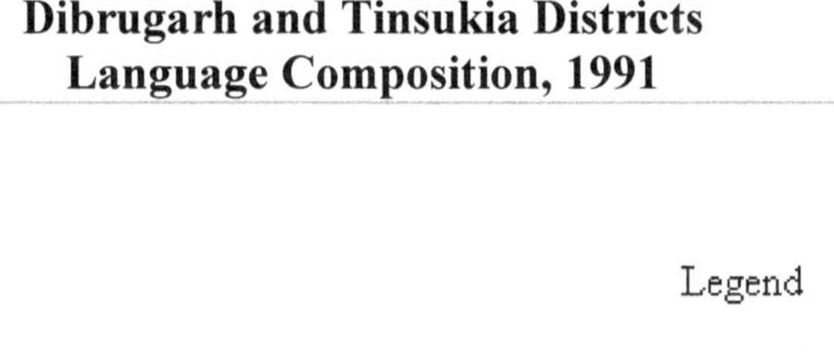

Fig-7.4

Distribution of SC and ST population:

The population distribution of scheduled castes and scheduled tribes is another social feature of Indian towns. The rural areas with a low literacy rate and low income are where the scheduled caste people are concentrated. The Scheduled Tribe population in the Dibrugarh and Tinsukia Districts in 1961 is depicted in the table (7.8) that follows.

Table-7.8
Dibrugarh and Tinsukia Districts
Scheduled Tribe Population in 1961

S.T	Male	Female	Total
All tribes total	48,935	45,357	94,292
Rural	48,470	45,025	93,495

Urban	465	332	797
Boro kachari	2,696	2,944	5,640
Deori	1,311	1,115	2,426
Kachari including Sonowal	23,726	20,947	44,673
Lalung	1,168	923	2,091
Mech	1,412	1,656	3.068
Mishing	17,276	16,596	33,872
Rabha	1,346	1,176	2,522

Source:- Gazetteer of India Assam state, Lakhimpur District 1976

According to the 2001 census, there was 6.77 percent scheduled caste residents and 13.30 percent scheduled tribal residents in each district. Up to 72% of the scheduled caste population in the area resides in rural areas, while 28% does so in urban areas. Similar statistics apply to scheduling tribes, where 93% of residents reside in rural locations and 7% do so in urban ones.

Table-7.9
Dibrugarh and Tinsukia Districts
SCs and STs Population of Urban Centres

Urban Centres	1991				2001			
	SC		ST		SC		ST	
	Male P.C.	Female P.C.	Male P.C.	Female P.C.	Male P.C.	Female P.C.	Male P.C.	Female P.C.
Tinsukia.	3.10	2.22	0.38	0.35	3.11	2.57	0.38	0.31
Doom Dooma.	2.15	1.76	0.39	0.55	2.92	2.72	0.43	0.47

Makum.	1.48	1.00	0.42	0.34	3.51	3.36	0.47	0.31
Margherita.	2.93	2.91	0.29	0.25	2.21	2.11	0.42	0.45
Digboi	3.52	2.98	1.05	0.83	2.72	2.56	1.17	1.01
Chabua.	1.28	0.79	0.33	0.31	1.52	1.20	0.27	0.26
Dibrugarh.	3.77	3.37	1.63	1.36	3.42	3.20	1.53	1.51
Duliajan.	3.85	3.02	1.71	1.27	2.45	2.14	1.80	1.62
Naharkatia.	3.0	2.46	3.86	3.98	5.44	4.25	7.82	7.47
Namrup.	1.81	1.21	2.62	2.39	2.18	1.69	3.33	3.01
Moran.	-	-	-	-	0.44	0.37	1.89	1.83

Source: Census of India,1991 and 2001 Primary Census Abstract, Population Tables

Naharkatia (9.69) has the largest percentage of South Carolina residents, while Moran Town has the lowest percentage (0.81). The SC population may not have relocated to the same degree, which is a significant component of meaning; the same explanation may apply to other places as well. According to the table no. 7.16, the Naharkatia town has the greatest ST population at 15.29, followed by Namrup town at 6.34, Moran town at 3.72, Duliajan town at 3.42, Dibrugarh town at 3.04, and Digboi TC at the lowest (0.34). The neighbouring town's population is likewise minuscule. The biggest percentage of SC and ST residents will represent the area's social development. According to table 7.9 (fig.7.5), the variable proportion of SC and ST residents in each town can be attributed to the various socio-economic backgrounds of the area.

Dibrugarh and Tinsukia Districts
SCs and STs Population (in P.C.) of Urban Centres

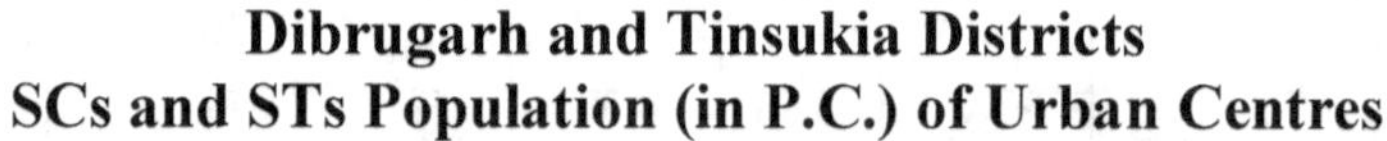

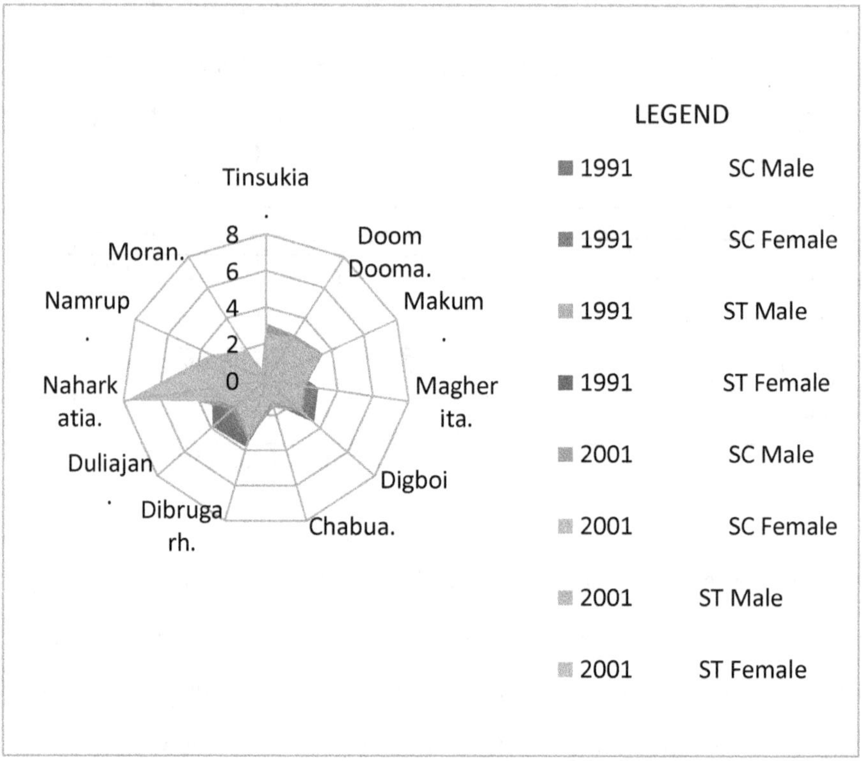

Fig-7.5

The density of Houses:-

One of the social parameters that shows the amenities of housing as well as the economic state is the density of dwellings. By dividing the number of homes by the area, the number of homes per square kilometer is determined (table 7.10 & fig 7.6). Chabua Town (3,377) has the most dwellings per square kilometer, followed by Duliajan (2,617) and Tinsukia (2,090). All of these municipalities registered a housing density of above 500, with

Moran having the lowest density (338). The highest density was found in Duliajan (1,821), followed by Tinsukia (1,509) and Dibrugarh (1,509) in 1991. (1,323). The density of housing increases as population density climbs. But it's a measure that's relative. It makes no mention of urbanization, which is related to the lack of land area in these high-density settlements.

Table -7.10
Dibrugarh and Tinsukia Districts
The density of Houses Per km² in Urban Centres

Towns	Areas	1991		2001	
		No. of houses	The density of houses/ km²	No. of houses	The density of houses/ km²
Tinsukia	10.54	13,948	1,323	22,029	2,090
Doom Dooma	4.30	2,685	624	3,671	854
Makum	3.68	2,268	616	2,912	791
Magherita	4.70	4,253	905	4,874	1,037
Digboi	17.47	6,982	400	7,489	430
Chabua	0.94	1,043	1,110	3,174	3,377
Dibrugarh	15.5	23,383	1,509	27,060	1,746
Duliajan	2.11	3,843	1,821	5,522	2,617
Naharkatia	5.34	2,848	533	2,980	558
Namrup	5.22	4,711	902	4,571	876
Moran	4.00	677	169	1,352	338

Source: Census of India,1991 and 2001 Primary, Census Abstract, Population Table.

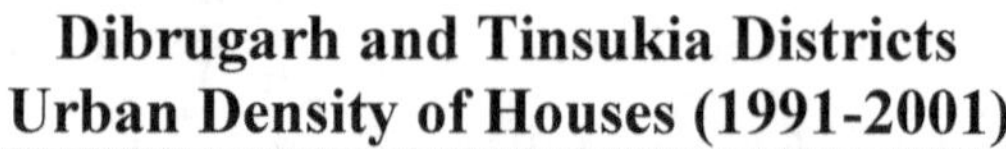

Dibrugarh and Tinsukia Districts
Urban Density of Houses (1991-2001)

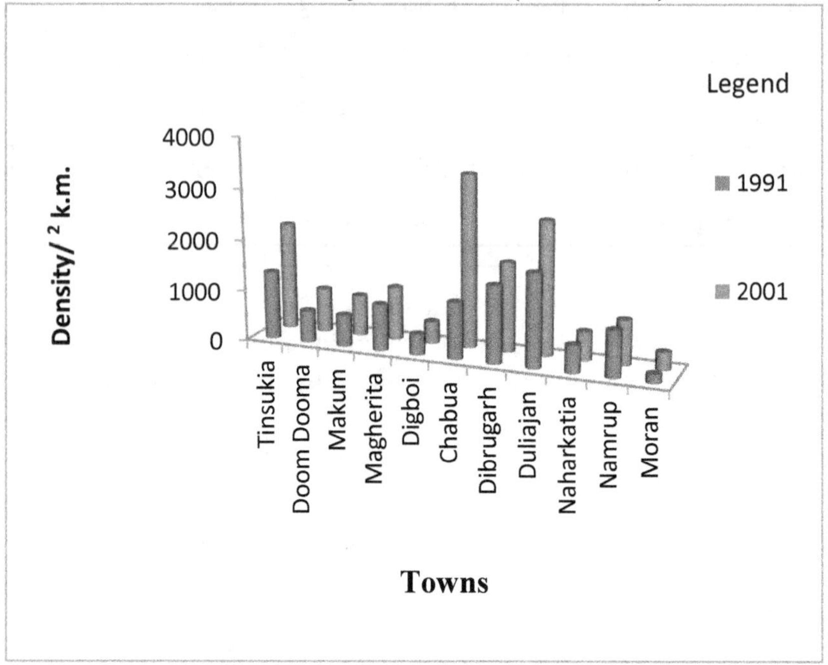

Fig -7.6

Person per Household:

The number of people per household, or the urban occupancy rate per house, is computed to clarify the house/population ratio, or the social structure of urban areas, as represented in the quality of housing, the residential environment, and house sizes (Rao & Simhadri, 1999). It is a measure used to determine the social dimension of urbanisation. A key sociological indicator of urbanisation, the household structure reveals information on the standard of living and house size. In the urban parts of the Dibrugarh and Tinsukia districts, there are six people per home. Tinsukia Town has the most residents (6), followed by

Digboi (6), Dibrugarh Town (6), Chabua (6), etc. Namrup (4%) has the least number of residents (6). (2001). Between the minimum value and the maximum value, there is not much fluctuation. Chabua town had the highest occupancy rate in the census year 1991 (table-7.11) with a (6), followed by Digboi town (6). One characteristic of the social dimensions of urbanisation is this fluctuation over time. This is a blatant sign that there aren't many people living in each family in the Dibrugarh and Tinsukia districts' urban core.

Table-7.11
Dibrugarh and Tinsukia Districts
Urban Occupancy Rate
(Number of Persons Per Household 1991-2001)

Towns	1991	2001
Tinsukia.	5	6
Doom Dooma.	5	5
Makum.	5	5
Magherita.	5	5
Digboi	6	6
Chabua.	6	6
Dibrugarh.	5	6
Duliajan Oil.	4	4
Naharkatia.	5	5
Namrup.	4	4
Moran.	-	5

Source: Census of India,1991 and 2001 Primary
Census Abstract, Population Tables

Literacy and Education :

The town's vibrant population is reflected in the high literacy rate. The whole town's female literacy rate has increased (table-7.12). An important sociological characteristic of urbanisation is the percentage of literate women. It is a reliable indicator of a region's degree of urbanisation. Increased literacy rates give an indirect indication of how urbanised a region is. The level of development and literacy rates are positively correlated (Chandna,1986). In 2011, Namrup Town had the greatest female literacy rate (90.88) and the highest male literacy rate (95.06). Despite having the most population in the districts, Dibrugarh Town ranks sixth for female literacy. Namrup has the greatest rate of female literacy, followed by Duliajan, Moran Town, Digboi, etc. Women's literacy rates are the lowest in Makum and Doom Dooma. Overall, male literacy rates are significantly greater than female literacy rates (table-7.12).

Table -7.12
Dibrugarh and Tinsukia Districts
Urban Sex-wise Literacy Rate (in %)

Years →	1991		2001		2011	
Towns	Male	Female	Male	Female	Male	Female
Dibrugarh	83.51	76.81	89.78	84.27	92.19	87.14
Chabua	87.52	70.18	94.38	84.23	82.63	74.68
Duliajan	89.92	83.47	95.73	88.68	97.24	92.18
Moran	91.31	82.24	91.21	86.46	92.51	87.53
Naharkatia	79.94	71.88	91.07	82.20	92.52	83.75
Namrup	89.47	84.82	95.06	90.88	95.79	91.78
Doom Dooma	74.24	62.52	84.61	72.84	90.47	82.23
Makum	75.16	63.07	82.28	70.45	85.21	75.09
Tinsukia	83.20	77.07	88.61	81.00	91.98	92.82

| Digboi | 93.46 | 76.99 | 92.17 | 85.16 | 94.90 | 88.23 |
| Margherita | 83.40 | 69.88 | 89.47 | 78.21 | 91.82 | 84.24 |

Source: Based on Census of India,1991, 2001, and 2011 Primary Census Abstract, Population Tables

The evolution of occupations over time and space:

The strength and diversity of occupational structure are crucial to the socio-economic success of an urban area. As a demographic attribute, the occupational structure of an urban centre is very important. Development should be boosted by a higher proportion of the working population.

Table -7.13
Dibrugarh and Tinsukia Districts
Urban Workforce Structure, 2001 and 2011

Towns	2001				2011			
	Main Workers	Marginal Workers	Total Workers	Non Workers	Main Workers	Marginal Workers	Total Workers	Non Workers
Dibrugarh	31.31	1.68	32.99	67.00	32.67	5.18	37.85	62.14
Chabua	45.05	2.64	47.69	52.31	29.56	4.49	34.05	65.95
Duliajan oil	29.74	1.22	30.95	69.05	30.89	3.63	34.52	65.48
Moran	29.81	6.16	30.72	69.28	30.69	1.92	32.61	67.39
Naharkatia	31.22	1.75	32.96	67.04	32.14	4.93	37.07	62.93
Namrup	29.05	0.97	30.01	69.99	31.92	7.52	39.44	60.56

Doom Dooma	30.76	1.87	32.63	67.37	28.88	5.43	34.31	65.69
Makum	29.83	3.64	33.44	66.56	27.91	7.24	35.16	64.84
Tinsukia	32.70	2.64	35.34	64.66	33.56	3.56	37.13	62.87
Digboi	31.02	1.15	32.17	67.84	32.88	3.54	36.42	63.59
Margher ita	28.77	2.38	31.15	68.85	29.90	5.94	35.84	64.16
Ledo Town	26.60	1.74	28.34	71.66	28.68	3.76	32.44	67.56
Chapakh owa					30.11	8.43	38.54	61.46

Source: Census of India 2001 and 2011 Town Directory, Assam

Dibrugarh and Tinsukia Districts
Urban Work force Structure, 2001 and 2011 (in P.C.)

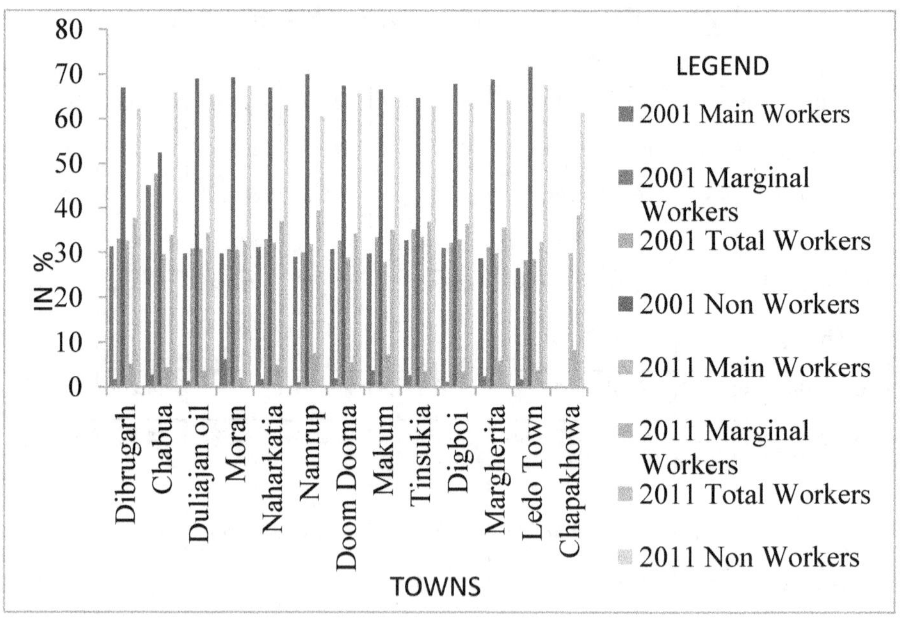

Fig-7.7

The Dibrugarh and Tinsukia Districts exhibit a low rate of labour force participation relative to their respective populations (table-7.13 & fig.7.7). According to the 2001 census, Chabua Town had a high participation percentage of main workers (45.05%), whereas Ledo Town had a low participation rate of main employees (26.60%). Nevertheless, in 2011, Digboi had the largest proportion of main workers (32.88%), and Ledo Town had the lowest (13.98). Therefore, the Marginal Workers' Participation Rate is highest in Chapakhowa Town (8.43%) and lowest in Moran Town (1.92%) in 2011 and highest in Chapakhowa Town (8.43%) and lowest in Namrup (0.97%) in 2001. Table 7.14 shows that less than 1% of urban workers are employed in the agricultural sector, which has been used as a major index to identify an urban settlement, whereas more than 99% of urban workers are employed in non-agricultural sectors.

Table -7.14
Dibrugarh and Tinsukia Districts
Distribution of Urban Workers, 2001 and 2011 (in%)

Towns	Agricultural Sector in %		Non-Agricultural Sector in %	
	2001	2011	2001	2011
Dibrugarh	0.48	0.83	99.5	99.2
Chabua	0.69	1.32	99.3	98.7
Duliajan oil	0.44	0.43	99.6	99.6
Moran	0.74	0.93	99.3	99.1
Naharkatia	3.13	2.18	96.9	97.8
Namrup	0.11	10.02	99.9	90.0
Doom Dooma	0.56	0.80	99.4	99.2
Makum	1.73	2.29	98.3	97.7

Tinsukia	0.66	0.90	99.3	99.1
Digboi	1.01	0.64	99.0	99.4
Margherita	0.88	0.79	99.1	99.2
Lido Town	2.10	0.89	97.9	99.1
Chapakhowa	-	20.05	-	79.9

Source: Based on Census of India 2001 and 2011 Town Directory, Assam

India classified the working population into nine categories. Census of India (1991), (i)agriculture (ii) agricultural labour (iii) livestock (iv) mining and quarrying (v) manufacture other than home industry (vi) building (vii) trade and commerce (viii) transportation, storage, and communications (ix) and other services. Figure 3.9 shows a Ternary Diagram of Mitra's (1967) representation of the spatial structure of the town's functional classification in 1991. Here,seven groups of workers are classified into three major non-agricultural categories as indicated below leaving aside the agricultural two categories.

Group	**Erstwhile Industrial Categories**
A Industry	iii ,iv, v and vi
B Trade and	vii and vii
Transport	
C Services	ix

Here, seven groups of workers are classified into three major non-agricultural categories as indicated below leaving aside the agricultural two categories.

Table -7.15
Dibrugarh and Tinsukia Districts
Urban Occupational Composition, 1991

S.L No.	Towns	Workers in Percentage		
		Industry (A)	Trade and Transport (B)	Services (C)
1	Dibrugarh	23.4 %	45.3 %	31.2 %
2	Digboi	48.4%	35.2 %	17.2 %
3	Doom Dooma	21.4 %	54.4 %	21.1 %
4	Duliajan	50.4 %	12.8 %	36.5 %
5	Namrup	59.7 %	16.0 %	22.3 %
6	Chabua	53.7 %	54.0 %	22.5 %
7	Naharkatia	31.8 %	43.9 %	18.0 %
8	Tinsukia	25.9 %	49.5 %	21.3 %
9	Margherita	42.9 %	36.3 %	17.5 %
10	Makum	42.7 %	30.5 %	17.4 %

Source: Calculated by the author based on Census of India, 1991 Town Directory Series- 4, Assam

Dibrugarh and Tinsukia Districts
Ternary Diagram Showing
Occupational Structure of Urban Centres, 1991

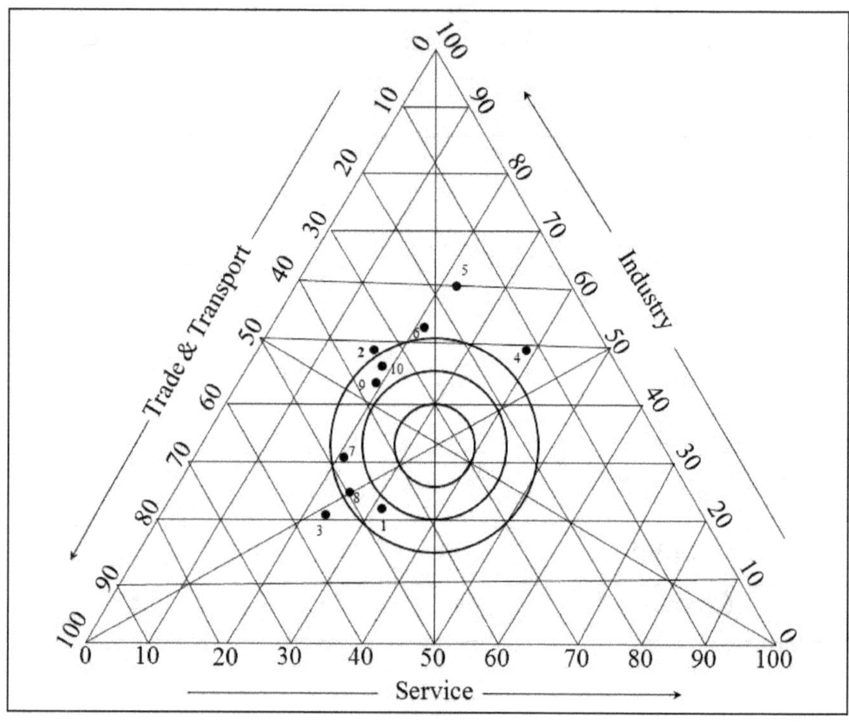

Fig – 7.8

From the above discussion, the towns of Dibrugarh and Tinsukia
Districts are classified as given below:

Towns	Group
Duliajan, Namrup, Chabua	Highly accentuated industry, low trade & transport, medium service
Naharkatia, Margherita, Digboi,	Highly & moderately accentuated industry, low service, medium trade &

168

Makum	transport
Tinsukia	Highly & moderately accentuated, trade & transport, low service,medium industry
Dibrugarh, Doom Dooma	Highly & moderately accentuated trade & transport,medium service, low industry

The information provided above demonstrates that the urban centres in the Dibrugarh and Tinsukia Districts lack a distinct functional classification. As a result, the districts lack any well-balanced urban centres.

Impact of Urbanisation on Occupational Change

The population of Dibrugarh and Tinsukia Districts has undergone a deep influence of occupational shift under urbanization from subsistence peasant economy to a mixed subsistence, industrial and commercial one over time and space. The tea industry along with other industries built up later on the basis of mineral and forest resources in the region and produced a diversity of job options for the individual which has an impact on diversification of the economy of the districts. The process of urbanization in the districts is mainly a movement of people in to both industry and service sectors from agricultural activities. It may be expected that with the development of manufacturing, construction, trade and commerce and transport and communication the structure of labour-force became change predominantly from agricultural towards manufacturing and services. The proportion of people employed in agricultural activities fell down substantially below 30 percent with the increasing employment in secondary and tertiary sectors in general laying down ground for urban development in the districts.

Bibliography and References:

Acharyya, N.N. (1966): *History of Mediaeval Assam*-Duttta, Barua and company, Guwahati.

Alvi, Zamir (1995): *Statistical Geography Methods and Applications* – Rawat Publications.Jaipur and New   Delhi.

Armstrong and Mc.Gee, T.G. (1986): *Theatres of Accumulation Studies in Asian and Latin American Urbanization*, Methuen, New York.

Aurousseau, M. (1924): "Recent Contributions to Urban, Geography : a review, *Geographical   Review* 14, 444.

Baransky, N. (1981): *Selected Works in Geography*, Progress Publishers, Moscow.

Bartholomew, H. (1955): *Landuses in American Cities*, Harvard U.P.,p26. Cambrige.

Barua, B.K. (1969): *A cultural History of Assam.vol-1* -Lawger's Book Stall, Gauhati

Berry B.J.L. (1971) – "Comparative Factorial Ecology" – *Economic Geography* (Supplement) P. 47.

Bhagabati, A.K.and Kar, B.K. (1999): *Survey of Research in Geography on N.E.India* (1979-1990): -Regency Publications, Guwahati.

Bhagabati, A.K, Bora, A.K, Kar, B.K (2001):Geography of Assam,(ed) Rajesh Publications. New Delhi-2 pp 3,28

Bhattacharya, B. (1979): *Urban Development in India since Pre-Historic Times*-concept publishing company, New Delhi.

Bhattacharyya, N.N. (1980) "Settlement system of N.E. India" in *North Eastern Geographer* Vol XII No. 1 and 2 G.U.

Bhattacharyya, N.N. (1971) "Urban Morphology of Gauhati *North Eastern Geographer* vol 2, No. 2 Guwahati University P.P. 141-150.

Bhuyan, S.K. (1949-50): *Anglo Assumes Relations* Historical and Antiquarian Studies Gauhati. Assam

Bogue, Donald, J.and Zachariah, K.C. (1962): "Urbanization and Migration" in Roy Tuner's *India's Urban Future* (ed), Oxford Univ. Press. Bombay

Borah, J. (1985): *Spatial Structure of Urban Influence in the Neighbouring Area of Gauhati*, Inter India Publications, New Delhi.

Borpujari, H.K. (1963): *Assam In the Days of company Historical and Antiquarian Studies* –Gauhati.

Borooah, G.L. (1985) *Population Geography of Assam; A study of Dibrugarh district*, Mital Publications Delhi- P- 119.

Borpujari, H.K. (1986): *The American Missionaries and North-East India (1836-1900 AD)* A Documentary Study-United publishers USA distributors East India Book company

Bose, A-(1973) *Studies in Indian urbanization 1901-1971*,Tata Mac Graw Hill Publishing C.O. Ltd. Bombay P-3.

Buragohain, P.L. – (1996) *A Study in population Geography*, "The Ahom population of Assam", Unpublished Ph.D. dissertation.

Carter, H. (1974): *The Study of Urban Geography*, Edward Arnold, London P-171.

Census of India (1991): Series –4 Assam, part –II B *Primary Census Abstract, General Population Scheduled Casts & Scheduled Tribes –* Service director of Census operation India.

Census of India (1991): Series-4 part ix-A *Assam, Town Directory* Director of Census operations. Assam.

Census of India 1901-1961 VOI III, Assam part I and Part II, GoI

Census of India 1991, 2001 primary census abstract series 4 & 19 Assam, GoI

Census of India 1971, Series & Assam part II-A General Population Table, GoI

Census of India 1971 Series 3 Assam part X-A & Town Directory. – Lakhimpur District.

Census of India 1981 Part XIII-A Village & Town Directory – Dibrugarh –XI

Census of India 2011 provisional population totals, paper 2, Volume 2 of 2011 Rural- Urban Distribution Assam Series 19

Cenzone, M. R.G. (1960) *The Plan Analysis of an English City Centre*, 'In Norkorg (Ed), Proceedings of I.G.U. Symposium on Urban Geography' e.w.k. Gleerup, Lund.

Champakalakshmi, R. (1996): *Trade, Ideology and Urbanization in South India 300 B.C to A.D.1300*, Oxford Univ. Press.

Chandna, R.C. (2006): *Geography of Population Concept Determinants and Pattern-* By Kalyani publishers.
Chatterjee, S.k (1974): Kirata Janakriti, Gauhati, p35

Cooley, C.H. (1894): "The Theory of Transportation,"*Publications of the American Economic Association*.

Crowe, P.R. (1938): "On Progress in Geography"- *Scottish Geographical Magazine*

Das, A.K. (2007) : *Urban Planning in India* –Rawat Publications, Jaipur.

Das, M.M. (2006): *Population resources and development a Geographical perspective* -N.E. India Geographical Society EBH Publishers Ghy. p150

Devi, Sobhabati Ch. and Singh R.P. – (1986)- "The Trends and patterns of Urbanization in Manipur" *N-Eastern Geographer* vol 19, No 1 & 2.

Dickinson, Robert E. (1964):*City and Region- A Geographical Interpretation,* London, Routledge & Kegan Paul.
Doniwal, H. K. (2009) *Urban Geography* P-89 Published by GNOSIS Delhi-110092.

Dutta & Dutta (1901 Rep 1976) *Assam District Gazetteers,* Guwahati, Assam.

Garrison, W.L. – (1965), *Applicability of Statistical Influence to Geographical Research,* Geographical Review. P- 427-429.

Garniner, J.B, Chabot, G (1967) *Urban Geography,* Longman Group Ltd, London, P288.

Ghosh, A. (2003 ed): *Urban Environment Management local Government and Community Action. Urban studies series no –* 7.Published for Institute of social sciences & Friedrich Ebert stfitung - Concept Publishing Company New Delhi-110059. p138

Gibbs, Jack, P. (ed) (1961): *Urban Research Methods,* Princeton, D.Van Nostrand Co. P100

Goode, J William, Paul K. Hatt (2006): *Methods in Social Research –* Surjeet Publications

Goswami, P.C. (1994): *The Economic Development of Assam* –Kalyani Publishers Ludhiana-New Delhi.

Govt. of Assam, Statistical Hand Book, Assam (2006, 2008): Directorate of Economics and Statistics , Guwahati.

Govt. of Assam, The Assam Gazette (1993,2007,2010): Urban Development Department.

Govt. of India (1976, Rep.1999): Gazetteer of Insdia, vol. A, Assam State Lakhimpur District pp 109, 231, 481.

Hall, T. (1998): *Urban Geography* routledge contemporary human geography series-Routledge 11 New fetterlane, London C 4P 4EE.

Hassert, K (1907): Dte Stadte Geographical Betrachect, Leipzig.

Herbert, D.T and Johnston R.J. (1978): *Geography and the Urban Environment progress in Research and Applications.* -Thomson Press (India) Limited New Delhi and Printed and bound in Great Britain by the Pitman Press ltd. Bath.

Huggett, J. Richad & Meyer, J.R (1981): *Geography: Theory in Practice Book one Settlements* –Harper & Raw Publishers

Hunter, W.W. (1879): *A statistical account of Assam* VOL II B.R. Publishing corporation, Delhi 1975 (Rep) - P-364.

Hoyt, H. (1939): *The structure and Growth of Residential Neighbourhoods in American Cities.* Federal Housing Administration, Washington.

Hurd, R. (1903): "Principles of City land Values", *New York Record and Guide.*

Jadav C.S. (1986) – *New Directions in urban Geography.* "Perspectives in Urban Geography volume I" Concept publishing company – New Delhi

Jha, V.N. (2006): *Small Towns and Regional Development,* Rajesh Publications, New Deldhi-110002 p152

Johnson, W.(1971):*Urban Residential Pattern,* Bell, London.
Knowles, R & Warcing, J (1976): Economic and Social Geography, Rupa & Co, Krishan,G. (1979): *Urban Geography-*

A Survey of Research in Geography, I.C.S.S.R, Allied Publishers, Bombay.

Mahmood, A.(1986) : Statistical Methods in Geographical Studies (ed),Rajesh Publications, New Delhi-110002

Mandol R.B. and Peters G.L.(1988) – *Urbanization and Regional Development.* Concept publishing Company New Delhi.

Mayer, Harold M. and Clyde, F.Kohn (1967): *Readings in Urban Geography* (ed), Central Book Depot, Allahabad

Misra, R.P. (1998): *Urbanization in India,* Regency Publications.

Mitra, Asok (1967): Internal Migration and Urbanisation in India, office of the Registrar General, pp.36-81.

Mudiar, K.K and Das M.M. (1978) – "Spatio temporal charge in the socio cultural level in Assam." – The North Eastern Geographer – Vol X No 1 & 2.

Murphy, R.E. (1966): *The American city:-An urban Geography*, Mc Graw Hill Book, company, New York, P 369.

Nelson, Howard J. 1955. – *"A service classification of American Cities."* Economic Geography Vol – 31.

Northam, R.M.(1975): *Urban Geography*, john wiley and Sons, New York, P.254.

Olsson, Gunnar (1940): "Stockholm- its Structure and Development,"*Geographical Review,*Vol-30.

Pemberton, R. B (1832): *The Eastern Frontier of British India* (supplement), The Government of Assam in the Department of Historical and Antiquarian Studies,Gauhati, Assam. I.D.Press,Calcutta-6

Phadke, V.S, and Guha S.B. (2007): *Urbanization, development and Environment (ed)*-Rawat publications.

Prasad, B.K. (2003): *Urban Development: A New perspective –* Sarup and Sons. New Delhi –11002.

Rai, R.k ; Singh, Surendra ; Nayak, D.K.and. Mipun, B.S.(2001) (ed) *:Environment Resources and development.*-The Geographical society of North-Eastern Hill Region (India) dept of Geography N.E. Hill University of Shillong –14.

Ramachandran, R. (1999): *Urbanization and Urban Systems in India,* OUP, New Delhi.

Ramakrrishna, G.(1999) " Urbanization and Economic Growth in India" in *Indian Cities Towards next millennium,* Rawat Publication New Delhi. PP 101-108.

Rao, R.& Simhadri, S(1999 eds) *:Indian Cities Towards next millennium* Rawat Publications,Jaipur-302004 pp133-143-184-197

Rao, V.L.S.P. (1964): *Towns of Mysore* –State Bombay Asia publishing House.

Richard, A (1942): "Elements in Urban Fringe Pattern," *Journal of Land & Public Utility   Economics,* vol, xviii, pp. 169-83

Robinson, W.A (1841, 1875 Rep.): *Descriptive Account of Assam,* Sanskaran Prakashak, Delhi .

Sankar, U. (2001): *Population Pattern and Urban Development* –Rajesh publications-New Delhi-12 Stamford p72

Sharma, H.N.(1978): "Urban growth and spatial pattern of urban development in the   Brahmaputra valley Assam." *North Eastern Geographer* Journal of the N.E. India Geographical Society VOL X I No. 1 & 2 P- 31

Sharma, M.C. (1982): *Structural Analysis of the City of Gauhati-A Geographical Study*, Naya Prakash, Calcutta.

Sharma, S. (2002): *Social Transformation in Urban India*, Dominant Publishers and Distributions, New Delhi.
Shevky, E.and Bell, W. (1955): *Social Area Analysis*, Stamford Univ. Press,

Siddhartha, K. and Mukherjee, S. (2006): *Cities, Urbanizations and Urban Systems*, Kisalaya Publications, Delhi. p1

Singh, Kh.Y (1982) *"Imphal A Study in Urban Geography"* Unpublished Ph.D. Dissertation, G.U.

Singh, M.B. (1981) – Imphal 'A Study on urban geography unpublished Ph.D. Dissertation Utkal University, Bhubaneswar.

Singh, D.K. (1971) "Dibrugarh and its Environs A Study in Quantitative Analysis of the Urban landscape of the Region" unpublished Ph.D. Dissertation G.U.

Singh, B. (2007): *Urban Geography with Special Reference to Patiala*, Rajesh Publications, New Delhi.110002.pp 85,98

Singh, L. (2010): *Environmental Geography (ed)*-A PH publishing corporation New Delhi-110002.

Sing,L.R.(2005):*Fundamentals of Human Geography*-Sharda Pustak Dahwan,

Allahabad.

Sing, R .Y. (2002): *Geography of Settlements.* Prem Rawat for Rawat Publications-Jaipur.

Singh, U.B (1999): *Urban Governance in North Eastern Region,*-Gayan publishing House.New Delhi –110002.

Smails, A.E. (1946): The Urban mesh of England and Wales. *Transactions and Papers, Institute of British Geographers*,101.

Smails, A.E. (1967): *The Geography of towns,* London. P84

Smith, R.M.T. (1965) "Method and purpose in Functional Town Classification". Anmals of the association of American Geographers P- 539-548.

Sudhir, H. (2009) ed: *Urbanization in North East India. Issues and Concerns.* - Akansha publishing House. New Delhi –12.

Swain, A.K. D.C. (2005): *A Textbook of Population Studies*-Kalyani publishers-New Deldi-110002.

Taher and Ahmed (2001) – *Geography of N.E. India* – Mani Manik Prakash Guwahati.

Ullman, E.L. (1985). *The nature of Cities*, "Anmals, American Academy of Political and Social Science". P – 7-17.

Taneja,K.L (1971) *"Morphology of Indian cities"* National Geographical   society of India, Varanasi, p.145

Wingo, Lowdon Jr. (1961): "Transportation and Urban Landuse,"*Washington D C.,* Resources for the Future Inc.

Appendix-4.1
Dibrugarh and Tinsukia District
Growth of Urban Population in Percentage 1901-2011

Urban Centres	Year →	1872	1881	1891	1901	1911	1921	1931	1941	1951	1961	1971	1981	1991	2001	2011
Dibrugarh	Population	3,870	7,153	9,876	11,217	14,563	16,007	18,734	23,191	37,991	58,480	80,348	1,03,008	1,25,667	1,37,661	1,54,019
	Growth in %	–	84.8	38.1	13.7	29.7	9.9	17	23.8	63.8	53.9	37.4	28.2	22	9.5	11.9
Tinsukia	P						3,080	5,160	8,338	12,245	28,468	54,911	64,414	73,918	1,08,123	1,34,392
	G						-	67.5	61.6	46.9	132.5	92.9	17.3	14.8	46.3	24.3
Digboi	P										35,028	32,388	34,161	35,933	37,143	38,666
	G										-	-7.5	5.47	5.2	3.4	4.1
Duliajan	P											11,497	14,257	17,017	31,974	38,105
	G											-	24	19.4	87.9	19.2
Margherita	P											9,250	15,480	21,709	24,049	26,913
	G											-	67.4	40.2	10.8	11.9
Namrup	P											7,972	13,856	19,740	19,021	15,483
	G											-	73.8	42.5	-3.64	-18.6
Doom Dooma	P						1,162	1,900	2,177	3,099	18,192	10,510	12,815	15,121	19,806	21,469
	G						-	63.5	14.6	42.4	132.1	28.3	21.9	18	31	8.4
Makum	P											5,992	8,993	11,993	15,118	16,875
	G											-	50.1	33.4	26.1	11.6
Chabua	P										2,533	3,888	4,996	6,104	17,433	8,788
	G											53.5	28.5	22.2	185.6	-49.6
Moran	P														6,826	8,445
	G														-	23.7
Chapakhowa	P															10,320
	G															-
Ledo	P														15,335	16,811
	G														-	9.6
Naharkatia	P										8,877	10,774	12,913	15,052	15,523	18,924
	G										-	21.4	19.9	16.6	3.13	21.92

(Source : Census of India Series 3, Assam 1991, 2001, 2011 Town Directory)

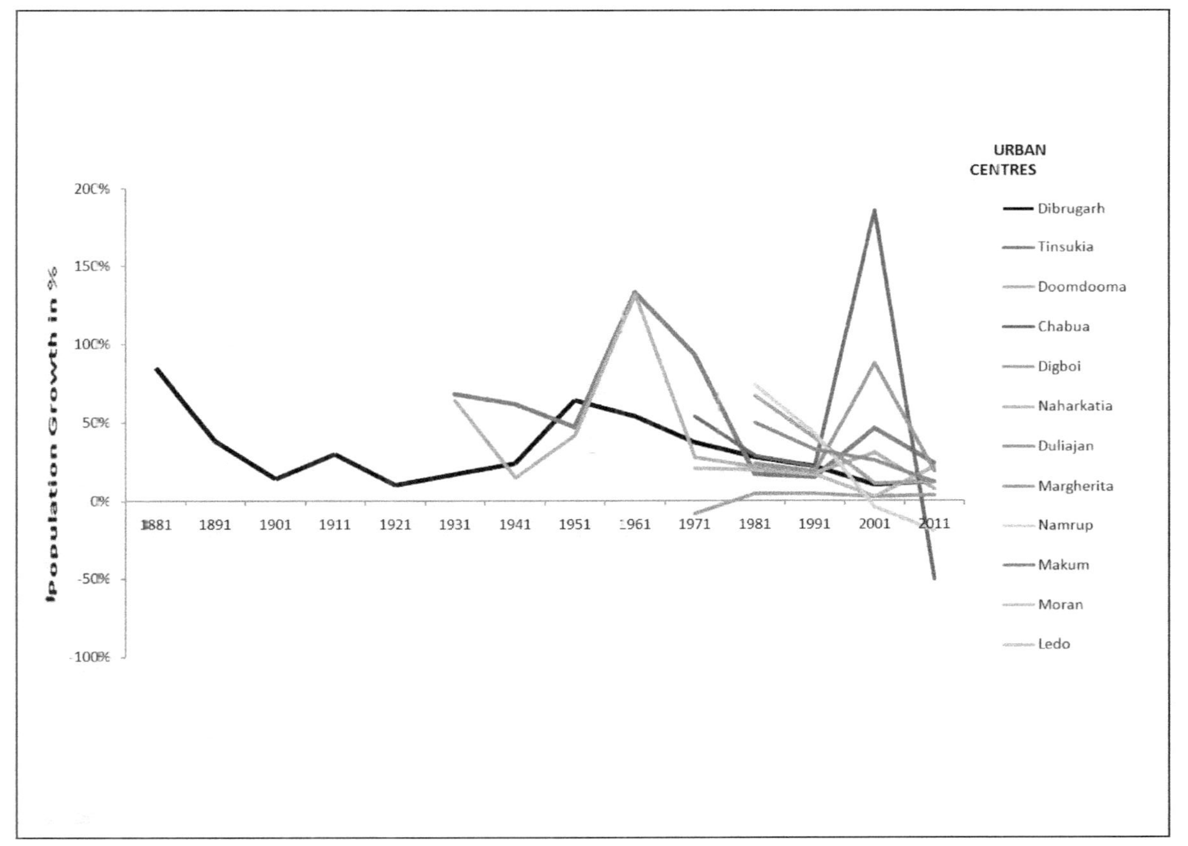

URBAN CENTRES
Dibrugarh
Tinsukia
Doomdooma
Chabua
Digboi
Naharkatia
Duliajan
Margherita
Namrup
Makum
Moran
Ledo
Population Growth in %
200%
150%
100%
50%
0%
-50%
-100%
1881
1891
1901
1911
1921
1931
1941
1951
1961
1971
1981
1991
2001
2011

Appendix- 6.1
Dibrugarh and Tinsukia Districts
Total Rural and Urban Migrants from Different States and Union Territories into Dibrugarh and Tinsukia Districts
1991- 2001

	States & Union Territories	1991				2001			
		Total Migrants	In % to Total migrants population	Total Rural Migrants	Total Urban migrants	Total Migrants	In % to Total migrants population	Total Rural Migrants	Total Urban migrants
1	Jammu & Kashmir	40	0.09	0	40	107	0.13	58	49
2	Himachal Pradesh	570	1.33	410	160	144	0.77	63	81
3	Punjab	1040	2.42	560	480	1241	1.46	325	916
4	Chandigarh	0	0	0	0	58	0.07	10	48
5	Uttaranchal	0	0	0	0	260	0.31	116	144
6	Haryana	800	1.86	560	240	1389	1.63	403	986
7	Delhi	50	0.12	10	40	320	0.38	125	195
8	Rajasthan	2500	5.83	1540	960	3071	3.6	885	2186
9	Uttar Pradesh	8000	18.65	5890	2110	14203	16.67	5950	8253
10	Bihar	20131	4695	16751	3380	38792	45.53	15390	23402
11	Sikkim	10	0.02	10	0	349	0.41	325	24
12	Arunachal Pradesh	420	0.98	260	160	2988	3.51	2263	725
13	Manipur	130	0.3	50	80	562	0.66	316	186
14	Mizoram	60	0.14	20	40	95	0.11	68	27
15	Tripura	2068	4.82	998	1070	2833	3.82	845	1988
16	Meghalaya	850	1.98	250	600	1131	1.33	462	669

17	Assam	0	0	0	0	0	0	0	0
18	West Bengal	3683	8.59	1142	2541	7132	8.37	2083	5049
19	Jharkhand	0	0	0	0	2421	2.84	2114	307
20	Chhattisgarh	0	0	0	0	275	0.32	250	35
21	Madhya Pradesh	130	0.3	90	40	756	0.89	540	216
22	Gujarat	180	0.42	100	80	229	0.27	75	154
23	Daman & Due	0	0	0	0	0	0	0	0
24	Dadra & Nagar Haveli	10	0.02	0	10	0	0	0	0
25	Maharashtra	120	0.28	70	50	401	0.48	146	255
26	Andhra Pradesh	1000	2.33	780	220	2585	3.03	859	1666
27	Karnataka	70	0.16	10	60	275	0.32	132	143
28	Goa	10	0.02	10	0	15	0.02	4	11
29	Lakshadweep	0	0	0	0	0	0	0	0
30	Kerala	210	0.49	90	120	600	0.7	294	306
31	Tamil Nadu	240	0.56	50	190	503	0.59	235	168
32	Pondicherry	0	0	0	0	4	0.01	3	1
33	Andaman & Nicobar Island	20	0.05	10	10	5	0.01	3	2
34	Orissa	420	0.98	330	90	1897	2.23	1254	643

Source: Census of India, Migration Table, Vol- I, 1991 – 2001

185

189